Shadow of a Myth

Shadow of a Myth

The Story of Che's Nephew in Cuba

Martín Guevara with Adrianne Miller

Wisdom Moon Publishing
2014

SHADOW OF A MYTH

THE STORY OF CHE'S NEPHEW IN CUBA

Copyright © 2014 Wisdom Moon Publishing, LLC

Copyright © 2014 information for photos on pages 70-73, indicated in place.

All rights reserved. Tous droits réservés.

No part of this work may be copied, reproduced, recorded, stored, or translated, in any form, or transmitted by any means electronic, mechanical, or other, whether by photocopy, fax, email, internet group postings, or otherwise, without written permission from the copyright holder, *except for brief quotations* in reviews for a magazine, journal, newspaper, broadcast, podcast, etc., or in scholarly or academic papers, *when quoted with a full citation to this work.*

Published by Wisdom Moon Publishing LLC
San Diego, CA, USA

Wisdom Moon™, the Wisdom Moon logo™, *Wisdom Moon Publishing*™, and *WMP*™ are trademarks of Wisdom Moon Publishing LLC.

www.WisdomMoonPublishing.com

ISBN 978-1-938459-37-5 (softcover, alk. paper)
ISBN 978-1-938459-40-5 (eBook)
LCCN 2014938981

TRANSLATOR'S PREFACE

I am a Cuban immigrant. I am one of the 14,600 children allowed to leave Cuba without my family during the Pedro Pan exodus, when our parents made the heart-wrenching decision to allow us to leave our families so that we could live in freedom. At the time I left Cuba, my father was a political prisoner. Prior to transferring to the Isla de Pinos prison, he was held at La Cabaña, an old Spanish fort where many prisoners were executed when Che Guevara was in charge.

Martin Guevara is Che Guevara's nephew.

My agreement to work closely with Martin in the translation of this work was not well received by many in the Cuban exile community. It was not well received by some of my close friends. How could I work with Che Guevara's nephew? What would my father, now deceased, say?

As we near the publishing of this translation I can tell you that this has been a magical process. Both Martin and I were able to leave behind our prejudices and learn to forge a working relationship and eventually a strong friendship that fostered a great deal of personal growth.

Translation is an art. It is not enough to know how to say a word in one language and repeat it back in another. Each language has a unique spirit that is sometimes almost impossible to convey in another. And each writer has a spirit that moves within that language in a unique way. As I prepared to do this work, I knew that in order to do it justice I had to understand how Martin and I used language. I had to merge with his spirit so that I could convey his words, his ideas, and his intention. This required that I get out of the way. That I not resist the flow, that I not judge or alter his words to suit my level of comfort, that I become a vessel through which his words could travel to you, the reader.

I come away from this work with a new respect for language, and with a new perspective of life, of the importance of tolerance and the sacredness of peace. I am grateful to Martin for this opportunity and I am proud to call myself his friend.

Prologue

I spent many years trying to run from the stigma of my uncle, Che Guevara. It wasn't easy. Che was like a torpedo in our family, like the conflagration of the big bang.

Beginning with his dramatic birth when he fought with all his might to live, while his parents hung on his every breath, nothing about him was ever ordinary. He was the oldest of five children and by far the most beloved by his mother who made no effort to conceal her feelings from his siblings. Che was spoiled. He was the North Star in the universe of his family.

My name is Martín Guevara. I am the son of Che's youngest brother, Juan Martín. Che was fourteen years old when my father was born and for all practical purposes it was he who was responsible for raising him. My father adored Che and tried to emulate him, but none of Ernesto and Celia's other children could ever hold a candle to Che in their parents' eyes and they, as well as the following generations of Guevaras, have spent a great deal of their lives trying to ascertain how to live under the shadow of a legend of myth-like proportions.

Che was a fearless child. From the way he challenged his body to overcome his severe asthma attacks to the reckless abandon in his play, he developed a penchant for living on the edge, for living in that space between the inhale and the exhale of a breath, a space that welcomed his restless spirit.

My uncle was loved but not over-protected. As a young child he would disappear for days and nights in the fields that surrounded the family's acreage in the countryside where he learned to survive without worrying anyone. The family expected he would come home victorious from his small adventures, and they were never disappointed. He was their little god.

Before the world transformed his bicycle with a small motor into a motorcycle, his parents saw in him the emerging hero. They helped expand the shadow that would one day make it difficult for his descendants to detect their own.

Latin Americans, perhaps because of their Spanish heritage or due to the initial isolation of those mostly soldiers and clerics who colonized its various countries, came to value their relatives in such a way that in most cases immediate family and extended family are just as important and deeply connected to one another. First and second cousins are as close to each other as brothers and sisters. The Guevara family shared that characteristic and more. We were like a clan, like a gypsy family, when Che arrived. He was the first member of the thirteenth generation of Guevaras in Argentina.

When Che became a revolutionary in a faraway country, when after his death he became an icon of socialist revolutionary movements and a world wide cultural icon, the Guevara family was forever changed.

Che's parents continued to adore him. One of his brothers, my father, tried to emulate him by joining a revolutionary movement in Argentina years after Che's death. His brother Roberto and his sisters Celia and Ana María, chose to live their lives in relative obscurity as they had lived their childhoods eclipsed by their older brother's brilliance.

Like his five children and my other thirteen cousins, I was expected to internalize my uncle's legacy, to become like my uncle Che. Herein lay the challenge. Which Che was I supposed to internalize?

When I met my uncle, he was already dead. I learned about him from my family, from the men who fought with him in the Sierra Maestra, and from those who had worked elbow-to-elbow with him during the years after the triumph of the Revolution. I learned about him from his wife and from his children, from textbooks and from the Cuban people. I learned about him from the heart of the father and brother who had loved him, from his writing, and from my own observation of a system of government that he had helped create, a system that engendered an unimaginably cruel repression of the Cuban people.

INTRODUCTION

Because of my relationship to an icon of the Cuban Revolution, I know well the misery hidden in the pretended moral superiority of "the left." It espouses the fight for the dispossessed, while robbing all people of their most basic human rights. I grew up in the company of lies and glaring contradictions between what the Revolution said it was, and its reality. The pressure I was under to become like Che in the midst of those circumstances became like an infection in my soul.

In my youth I had the courage to confront every injustice I observed on the island, inspired by my uncle's letter to the younger generation of the family to do just that. I decided early on that I only have one life and I want to live it my way and not as I was told I should live it, becoming a slave of the too-authoritarian Cuban authorities in exchange for the financial support of the Cuban Council of State—a support that might include a house with an ocean view.

I will always feel a certain kinship with the uncle who read Goethe, who read Rimbaud in French, with the sportsman who fought against his asthma, for the brilliant but undisciplined student, for the traveler who was capable of taking off his coat to give it to a less fortunate man on the highway. Yet I can find nothing in common with the man who slowly turned the beauty of his original intentions into cruel realities devoid of romanticism.

My uncle believed he owned a truth superior to the truth of any other human being. As a father, he declared he would protect the children of the world, yet he chose to fight a revolution and deprived his own children of his paternal warmth forever. I abhor the idea of solving a dispute by killing one's opponent, the insane effort of eradicating cannibalism by eating the cannibals. I trust that reconciliation and love for humanity can put us on a path towards building a world where all of us can live out our personal freedom as long as the rights of others are respected.

To that effect and as proof that a beginning is possible, two of us have come together to collaborate in this work: Adrianne Miller, born Yolanda López Capestany Miranda, and myself. Adrianne is an exquisite person, a writer and translator, who suffered the darkest days of the Cuban Revolution. She arrived in the United States alone at a young age during the little-known Pedro Pan exodus, having left her family behind and her father, Pablo Lopez-Capestany, condemned to twenty years in Isla de Pinos, a Cuban prison. I am the nephew of one of the men responsible for the Revolution that imprisoned her father, son of an Argentinian political prisoner and also an exile from my native country.

Our improbable collaboration was made possible through an unusual cascade of coincidences. Adrianne is currently writing her own memoir, *Ordinary Terror*. She is a psychotherapist living in Oregon and a close relative of Cuban dictator Gerardo Machado Morales, the fifth president of Cuba, who was deposed in 1933.

Both Adrianne and I were reluctant latecomers to Facebook, resisting pressure from our friends to take one more step into the social milieu of the twenty-first century.

One night, Adrianne was startled by the appearance on her Facebook list of suggested friends of several people with the last name of Guevara. Adrianne, who met my uncle in a unique set of circumstances described in her memoir, had a very strong reaction to the Guevara invasion into the sanctuary of her study. A few difficult days later, Adrianne learned that several Guevaras lived outside of Cuba and had been friends with the son of one of her childhood classmates.

What followed was an act of courage on both our parts. Adrianne had been very impacted by meeting Che, who had cast a shadow in her own life. She reached out to me and asked one question: "What has it been like for you to be the nephew of Che Guevara?" I learned that I had gone to school in Cuba with the children of Adrianne's childhood friend Rosita. Because we both trusted Rosita, we overcame our initial reticence to communicate, a reticence that no doubt would have kept us from ever engaging in dialog. It was what we chose to call a "veil of trust." It was this, based on our shared trust of Rosita, that allowed us to continue on this journey.

I had long felt the need to write, but it was Adrianne's question and my answer that began a dialog that engendered this book, a process I can only describe as magical.

Adrianne has given me the gift of knowing the Cuba that was, the Cuba that those of us who came later were never told about. Through her and her friends, I learned that Cubans were not always hungry, that the food in the old Cuba was abundant and varied in ways we never knew. That the poor could attend public schools anywhere on the island, schools we had been told did not exist; that the poor had access to medical care in neighborhood clinics staffed by competent physicians, many of whom had been educated in the United States. I learned that Cubans had hoped to be delivered from the cruelty of the Batista government, and not from the clutches of Imperialism, and that they had believed Fidel's promise to rule under the constitution of 1940 when they welcomed him with open hearts into their midst.

I had never heard about the Pedro Pan exodus, of which Adrianne was a part. More than 14,000 children were sent to the United States alone by parents desperate to give their children a chance to live in freedom. More than 90,000 other children who waited their turn to leave were impeded from doing so when Fidel stopped the program after the Cuban Missile Crisis.

My generation didn't know that Fidel had promised their parents they could join their children in exile only to renege on his promise after the children were gone, leaving many orphaned for years or forever, to forge a future alone but free in their new country.

Adrianne has never been back to Cuba and didn't know what life in Cuba was like after she left. I have been able to fill in at least part of the story she missed by leaving, and in my doing so, Adrianne has come to appreciate her family's decision to send her into exile alone and has felt a great sadness in the face of the senseless suffering of her people.

As our dialog continued, Adrianne became much more than my translator. She has been my companion on this journey, always by my side, listening, encouraging, and supporting me. We have come to understand each other and the demons that have plagued us. We have walked together in trust and truth, our words sometimes challenging each of us to open our minds and hearts further and by doing so, helping both of us to see Cuba from a more complete historical perspective. Most importantly, we have learned the extent to which the furtherance of peace and non-violence are important to both of us, and we are proud to do this work together hand-in-hand in what we hope will be a step toward reconciliation and a demonstration that shadows can be banished and enmities overcome. Our work has reminded us both that all of us that live in the New World are Americans. That anything that happens in any part of the Americas affects us all. And that the solutions to the problems we face lie in part in the willingness of the United States with all of the other countries of the Americas to recognize together their brotherhood as well as their diversity and autonomy.

Acknowledgments

The English version of my book would not have been possible without the selfless contribution of many people.

Our Skype sessions every Sunday for almost three years and our yearly visits to one another while we worked on this project took up valuable family time. We would like to thank my wife Patricia Vergara-Martín and my sons for their daily support and encouragement, as well as Adrianne's husband Ken Miller and Adrianne's daughter and sons. All of them gave up their Sunday afternoons with us for three years while we got to know one another, planned, and executed our project on Skype.

I would like to thank my friend Marcos Martinez for his encouragement of this project and Claudia Peiró of Infobae America for featuring my blog and helping me build a platform as an author.

I would also like to thank my beloved aunt, Celia Guevara Lynch, who despite her loyalty to and her love of her brother, my uncle Che, has loved and supported me all of my life.

Adrianne and I are grateful to our friends who have encouraged us as we walked this journey. We would like to thank the Writers in the Rafters, Adrianne's writers' group in Portland, who maintained confidentiality about the project and welcomed me with open arms during my visits to the U.S.

We particularly want to thank our publisher, Mitchell Ginsberg, for his interest in our work, for his dedication to its publishing, for the final edit of the work, his attention to detail, his sense of humor, and his commitment to making our book the best that it can be. Mitchell has been just the right partner at the finish line.

Chapter One

José Martí Airport, Havana Cuba

The day of my father's thirtieth birthday:

As I approached the bottom of the airplane's metal steps, my ten-year-old senses were assaulted by a sweet and humid heat that entered through my nose and brought forth the first drops of sweat from my temples. My parents, my younger brother and sister, and I were all rushed through customs and immediately escorted to two waiting vehicles. One was for us to ride in, and the other was full of people asking us how our trip had been and welcoming us to the island. Judging from the look one of the occupants of the car was giving us, they had also come to see if we were a kind of Chinese jar that had arrived by mistake or if indeed we were authentic members of the family they awaited. I noticed that all who came to greet us were dressed in olive green, and every one wore guns strapped to their waist. Something unusual was happening. We seemed to be important people, the kind of people worthy of being guarded with automatic weapons. Our bags were loaded in the trunk with unnatural speed. In a few moments our car took off speeding faster than any other car on the road, as we rode down Rancho Boyeros Avenue on the way to the city.

I couldn't stop staring at the plants that revealed themselves like a new universe. They were green from their roots up and everything that grew seemed to have more chlorophyll than it could contain. Some plants ended in vivid red flowers, others in yellow, yet others in blue. The air coming through the car window was laden with the scent of humidity combined with the aroma of flowers, wet grass, and decomposing leaves that make up the intoxicating smell of the tropics. The pedestrians were very distinctive because of their simple dress and because every two or three of them were of African descent. I had seen the first African man at the airport. He was on the tarmac seated on a luggage cart. I had fantasized about this moment for a long time. I had wondered if people of African descent had hair that was impossibly curly. I had only seen men of African descent, black men, on television series like *Daktari*.

We arrived at the hotel that would be our home for several years, although at the time I thought it would be our home for only a month. It was the Hotel Habana Libre. The hotel was a magnificent building. It had twenty-five floors in addition to some underground levels. The building occupied a whole city block. It had been built in 1958 by the Hilton Hotel chain. We entered through an impressive lobby with perfume-scented water fountains. A smiling employee approached and took our bags, and another brought us fruit juices I had never before tasted. I was startled when I caught sight of my cousins Juan and Rosario, who were part of our welcoming committee. We hugged one another, exchanged fists simulating boxers in the fighting ring, and agreed to meet later after we unpacked. My family was given two rooms facing the ocean on the fifteenth floor. The hotel, its location and its views, was nothing like any place I had ever seen before. Our room had an entry hall with a closet, a shoe holder, and a chest of drawers. Off the entry hall was an ample marble bathroom with a large tub. The bathroom was partitioned from the room by a wooden walkway with two twin beds, a desk, a TV stand, and a table that held a radio and various other electronic gadgets.

The Hotel's name had been changed from the Habana Hilton to the Hotel Habana Libre (The Free Havana Hotel) in 1959, when it housed the rebels that had occupied Havana. On this day I was told that among those rebels had been my uncle, my father's oldest brother. I had never met him and I had never heard him mentioned before, perhaps because the family was careful not to mention him in my presence, or perhaps they had referred to him by a different name. Or maybe at the age of ten, the oldest of three children, I had been too preoccupied in my own world to pay much attention to absent members of the family. My uncle's name was Ernesto Rafael Guevara, and he was affectionately referred to as "Che." I was told he had fought to save the world from hunger and misery and that he had died in combat to advance a war without barracks against an enemy that from that day on must become my own. I was told this, and given no time to think. I was told my uncle had died in 1967 in Bolivia and that the country we were in had been liberated by him and other men who shared in his fight against oppression. Among them had been his boss, the only one who had survived everything and everyone, Fidel Castro Ruz, who years later and for the rest of our lives we would refer to as "Guarapo." I was clearly instructed that after that moment I was no longer to call anyone "sir" or "ma'am," but "comrade."

From that moment on we would live in a new society where the new man was forged by sacrifice. As I listened, I hopped up and down on the bed to try out the great mattress springs. My father told me I had some new cousins who would come and play with me the next day. He told me they were Cuban, children of my new dead uncle. One emotion after another passed through me with barely time to take a breath between them!

When I stopped jumping on the bed and finished trying every one of the cold milk shakes the staff had brought in for us in metal pitchers, I took some Argentinian magazines out of the suitcase, put them on the night stand, walked to the bathroom, and I locked myself in. I needed to be alone to think about everything that had happened. I had always been inclined to feel sorry for the poor. I was a reader of Salgari's books, the sagas of El Corsario Negro (The Black Pirate) and Sandokán, because they both stood against injustice. Many times I had pretended to be a tiger of Mompracem with other children or by myself and fantasized that Sandokán praised me for my valor. I had just been told that I had an uncle more famous and at least as brave as Sandokán, who also fought against injustice. I felt that being related to him granted me some of my uncle's heroic virtues.

I contemplated the great vacation that awaited us. We would be taken to the countryside, to the ocean to sail, to play on beaches of fine white sand, and I would get to visit these places with my cousins. I was so excited! I left the bathroom, retrieved the magazines from the night table to share with my cousins, and asked for permission to go play with them. My cousins were also staying on the fifteenth floor. We spent the rest of the day talking about all the changes in our lives. We talked about our new relative, how important he was, how beautiful Cuba was, the new words we had to learn, the new cousins I would meet the next day, and we talked about all that kids talk about with the irreverence and humor so typical of children when dealing with serious subjects, with a logic devoid of conscience. My cousins took me to meet the salespeople in the hotel stores and showed me the pool, the playroom, the kids' park, and all the places where we could run. I went back to the room to freshen up after our visit and was ready when my father came to pick me up. It was time to eat. That night we had dinner on the twenty-fifth floor in the Sierra Maestra Restaurant. It was a fun dinner. The lights in the restaurant were dimmed and I could see a few lights illuminating the city through the huge windows. A pianist was playing waltzes. Before the day was over, I made another discovery, this time a culinary one: ruffle fillet and shrimp cocktail. We stayed up very late into the night, my parents with my uncles and aunts, and my brother, my sister, and I, with my cousins. The next day we went for a walk in the city. We walked down Twenty Third Street, the street where our hotel was located. The smell of sea-salt and ocean breezes filled the air with anticipation before we arrived at the Malecón. Once there, our eyes made contact with the bluest possible ocean wrapping itself around a reef, at the same time the tropical breeze embraced us.

It's easy to understand why hundreds of thousands of residents of Havana through the centuries wove their dreams of love and riches by the Malecón, as well as their songs of madness and resignation.

Later we climbed up the sidewalk by the Hotel Nacional, to the highest building in the city at that time, the Foxa building. All the time I was aware of experiencing a heat that was different than any heat I had ever been exposed to.

The heat in Havana rises from the ground. My mother had left the hotel with shoes that were apparently inadequate for long walks under that sun and humidity at the end of May. She and my father started to argue because they couldn't find a pharmacy where they sold Band-Aids so my mother could cover the small blister that had appeared on her foot. My mother refused to continue and another argument ensued that had little to do with the blister on her foot. We began the walk back to our room.

On the way we found a pharmacy that had no Band-Aids but did have adhesive tape. My mother asked the salesgirl if she might have some cotton she could use to cover her blister. The salesgirl went to find her a piece of cloth to use instead of cotton. It was the first time I saw two things that were typical of the city and of Cuba in general: the extreme shortage of goods and the human warmth of the people. Perhaps it would be impossible to bear the one without the other.

After a few days, we were acclimated to the new environment. The chefs of all five restaurants at the hotel knew us, as did Paneque, the man in charge of the swimming pool, all the elevator operators that we drove crazy with our constant trips up and down, the housekeeping staff of our floor, the staff that swept and cleaned the bathrooms, and even the cooks and the people who washed and ironed our clothes. They knew us, but we didn't always know them. The man that came into the lobby to collect cigarette butts must have known me because every time he saw me he acknowledged me with a nod of his head, before filling his pockets with the cigarette butts he found in the elevator ashtrays, prior to being escorted out by the security guards.

There are two hotel employees I will always remember: one is Willy, the captain of the Mezzanine Restaurant Sierra Maestra, who was the epitome of elegance. He had the air of a palace employee, the visage of a royal butler ready to serve at any moment. Sometimes when visiting the restaurant we would order Baked Alaska. The moment it was served the lights were turned off. The flames, fueled by the alcohol, would rise. No one could serve Baked Alaska like Willy.

The other employee was Eloísa, from the perfume store. All purchases made inside our hotel were charged to our room. Anytime we wanted anything we would order it and at the end of every month a government employee would make sure everything was paid for by the State. Even cigarettes could be purchased this way, but since my parents were given one hundred and twenty Cuban pesos per month for miscellaneous expenses, they insisted on paying cash for their cigarettes as a point of decorum. I was never able to tell the difference between putting something on a tab or paying with cash, as both were gifts from the State and both were provided to us by the labor of Cuban men and women with burnished skin and shirts pierced by the sun that shone mercilessly bright on the sugar cane fields. Breakfasts, decadent lunches, all of our snacks, the evening beers, the midnight drinks, and all of our guests' expenses, everything was put on a tab, except for the packs of cigarettes. One afternoon my mother gave me cash and asked me to go to the perfume shop downstairs and get her a bar of soap that was softer and had more perfume than the usual hotel small courtesy soaps. In the lobby there were three stores: one was a novelty shop filled with stuffed frogs playing drums, hats made of a palm native to Cuba called Yarey, bongos, machetes, and other souvenirs. One was a retail store that sold clothes, music, and photography supplies. Across the way, separated from the other stores by a beautiful fountain, was a perfume store.

I walked into the store, found the salesgirl, and explained to her what my mother wanted. Smiling, she wrapped a bar of soap in a piece of paper, handed it to me, and told me that a child could not sign the tab but that it was no problem. She said I should ask my mother to come later to sign for it. I told her my mother had asked me to pay cash, but she insisted I should have my mother come later. She asked my name and introduced herself.

She knew I was a nephew of Che's, and she talked to me about my uncle. She told me she had met him and that everyone there loved him. After a while, I left and got on the elevator, where I opened the package Eloísa had wrapped. The tag on the soap read "Atardecer." It was the first word I learned how to pronounce with the phonetically characteristic accent of a resident of Havana. I returned upstairs to tell my mother she needed to go talk with the salesgirl, and lay down for a while thinking about being a Guevara.

I am not certain if it was due to the many exiles and vicissitudes, the hostilities faced in taming the southern lands and being able to extract from them what was needed. Perhaps we possessed genes that made us particularly susceptible to family. Regardless of the reason, we always felt a special pleasure and a sensation of security in belonging to something greater than ourselves, in the company not only of brothers and sisters, but also of uncles and cousins. We had knitted our close relationships in the fields of Portela, in the city of San Francisco, and in my uncle Roberto's house during Christmas and New Year's Celebrations. Moving to Havana had not changed how we felt but instead appeared to intensify those feelings now that five more cool new cousins would be added to the mix.

Moving to Havana had not changed how we felt, but instead appeared to intensify those feelings now that five more cool new cousins would be added to the mix.

Chapter Two

The next day I woke early, unable to sleep after a restless night. It wasn't only the arrival on the island and my newfound dead uncle and his children that populated my dreams, but the memories of my beloved country and our almost surreptitious departure.

In April of 1973, my parents told me we were going to spend a month in Santiago de Chile. We would go visit some friends and tour the country. They promised we would cross the Andes just as San Martín did after liberating Argentina from the Spanish, on his way to join his friend O'Higgins to help him liberate Chile. O'Higgins waited for him on the other side of the mountain with fresh horses and warm food, and with a great desire to begin an exquisite revolution of independence—the kind of revolution with horses and swords that leave impressionable girls in the throes of love with their heroes. Like Gabriela, the girl who captured my heart from the moment I entered my school and whom I could not stop my eyes from seeking until the day I left. She didn't pay much attention to me unless I had Tutti Frutti bubble gum that she also loved. I had learned the art of seduction by imitating the tactics my father used with El Doradillo, his beloved horse.

It wasn't the parallel with the history of my country that filled me with excitement when contemplating our travels, but the prospect of traveling through the mountains, of seeing snow for the first time in great quantities. I would get to see condors and mountain deer from the window of the train. When I returned, everyone would have to believe that I had been next to Anconcagua, the highest mountain in the Americas, that I almost fed the birds of prey I got so close to, and that I managed to live through severe snowstorms. I had a right to exaggerate. I almost got more pleasure from the license to fib than from the possibility that what I imagined could actually happen. A year before our trip, an airplane had fallen in the Andes Mountains carrying a team of Uruguayan rugby players headed for a competition in Chile. They survived the cold and gained world attention for how they fought against hunger. When there was no alternative they had to make a decision: they ate their dead traveling companions. I remember the discussions among kids my age about whether they would eat one another to survive, and I don't remember one who doubted the students had done the right thing. At a young age there is less malice as well as fewer taboos.

On May third we left for the train station in Retiro where the long distance trains leave Buenos Aires, with five huge suitcases and two smaller ones for two adults and three children who were supposedly going to spend a few days among friends. My parents had sold everything they owned. I remember we had enough cash to last much longer than we would need for a luxury one-month vacation. That day was my tenth birthday and almost all my friends as well as my cousins, aunts and uncles, came to say goodbye to us at the station. I blew out the ten candles on a delicious chocolate cake right there on the platform as they all sang "Happy Birthday" to me in the midst of our good byes.

I am not sure if I remember my tenth birthday with sadness or warmth. But the memory of that day has always evoked strong emotions in me. Argentina, the smell of the metro, of sandwiches de Milanesa, the color gray and the mist that in Buenos Aires we call *"garúa"*; the pleasant cold air on my face that fall day in Retiro, a similar kind of day as the day I was born. I remember the brick on the Torre de los Ingleses across from the train station, the ten candles on the cake, a box of chocolates, the whistle announcing our departure, Juan Martín, the uncles, and my beloved childhood friend Silvina, waving goodbye to us outside the train in the bitter cold. And once on the train I remember the motion of the train, and the luxury of the car where I still want to stay, opening presents and eating chocolate. That night I turned on the light and ate a few more bars of chocolate. I lay on the bed gazing at the ceiling feeling totally free. It certainly didn't seem as if we would be going home in a month. We had gone on vacations before, but this one felt different to me. Perhaps it was my intuition or maybe it was the way I interpreted the total emptying of our home prior to leaving. It could have been the long good-byes I witnessed full of interminable embraces, or perhaps the fact that I had been allowed to take with me my whole car collection and Cocó, who had never gone on vacation with us before and now lay at the bottom of my suitcase. Something wasn't right, but I didn't want to dwell on it. When we arrived at the Andes Mountains the sun was making the snow sparkle. I got off the train with my brother and sister, and we threw snowballs at one another. We had to change trains and we had a two-hour wait. I spent the whole time walking in the snow. When the train came, the train that would take us down the mountain towards Chile, the firemen almost had to be summoned. I had crawled into a hole in the snow and I wouldn't come out. Ultimately, I did. We arrived in Santiago de Chile at night, in the middle of a general strike, during a time when Salvador Allende was in power. My father had to walk a few blocks to find a cab because there were none by the station. We waited in a well-lit corner near the station until my father appeared in a car that had seen better days and had no sign on it identifying it as a cab. We put some suitcases in the trunk and some on the roof of the car and climbed inside where we sat as tightly packed as sardines in a can.

The driver drove us all over Santiago. He was very courteous towards us while his meter ran up quite a tab. The problem was that not only were cabs scarce, but hotel rooms were, too, due to the number of fans that had come to the city to attend a South American soccer tournament. Back then we were much more relaxed about travel. Today one doesn't leave home without reservations for hotels and an itinerary. Maybe my parents were very relaxed about traveling and it had nothing to do with the times. I thought it was odd that if we were in Chile to visit friends we weren't staying at their house.

The sound of car horns filled the night. Groups of men carrying placards and making noise would suddenly appear in front of us forcing the driver to make sharp turns to avoid them. We spent quite a long time dodging protesters, looking for hotels and finding no available rooms, all while continuing to enrich our driver. We tried hotels all over Santiago, including very expensive and newer hotels like the Hilton, the most expensive of all, and could not find one vacant room. We had plenty of money but we were on the verge of spending the night under a bridge by the Mapocho River. When it became obvious that we were not going to find a vacant hotel room, the driver pulled up to a curb and he and my parents got out of the car and began to speak in low voices. They all came back looking somewhat relieved and a few minutes later we were going up the stairway of a huge old house. A very heavy woman in her nightgown and a thin man in a t-shirt, pants, and slippers, spoke to the chauffeur briefly and bid us welcome. The place had little to do with our joy in finding it. There were many spacious rooms with spider webs, where there were men and women staying. The couple showed us our room. It had a huge bed and everything smelled like moisture. The woman who gave us our key told us to go downstairs at ten o'clock to eat. When we arrived at the appointed time we found a long table where some women sat in their nightgowns, and we were served boiled chicken that still had feathers attached to it that the chicken had not used to fly away. I never forgot that chicken, the table, the owner in his not-quite-white t-shirt, or his smile, and I still remember the heavy-set woman and the younger women looking at us as if we were a rare species of insect. We ate hungrily, went up to our room, and slept stuck to our blankets and pillows. When I woke the next day, my father had just come into the room wearing a broad smile because he had found us a hotel room for fifteen days. I went to brush my teeth and on the way back to my room crossed a bedroom that smelled like people's sweaty bodies. When we left the occupants of the house said goodbye to us as if we were part of their family leaving on vacation. They helped my father load the suitcases on a cab and the man pocketed a few more escudos than what the clients paid him to sleep with their girls. We had spent the night in a brothel. A few very restful days of vacation followed in Chile. The small hotel where we stayed for fifteen days, the Miami, was more like a motel with one-story units. It was very pretty and welcoming. We stayed in a small two-bedroom suite with a living room. I took my car collection out of my suitcase and lined up my cars on the floor feeling as comfortable as if I had just arrived at my new home.

Our first outing in the city was on a gray, cold day. A steady breeze blowing from the Andes pleasantly caressed my face. The city had a river running through it that gave it character. It wasn't a wide river, but it is said that for centuries a ghost ship named Caleuche has traveled it. People are warned that seeing the ship is very dangerous as anyone who sees it is taken away in it; a very clever way of preserving the mystery. Finally we went to spend two days with my parents' friends. My parents had known them since secondary school. The couple had two sons and they lived in a beautiful part of the city. The home was brick, with an Old English tile roof. The living room had several levels and a large fireplace in front of which my parents and their friends spent many hours enjoying each other's company, laughing and sometimes defending their points of view very passionately. One afternoon while they talked, their oldest son and I went for a bike ride. He was a year younger than I. After riding through some beautiful tree-lined streets in their neighborhood for some time, I heard my parents calling me. Their voices were tense and I thought I should approach the house to find out what they wanted. Mountains surround Santiago and from that part of the city I could clearly see the picturesque mountaintops covered with snow as I pedaled my bike towards the house.

Before I could reach my parents and our hosts I fell off the bike. I got back on the bike and again I fell, this time landing on my side. This was a residential street without much traffic, but the pavement was as hard as that of any street. I decided to push my bike the rest of the way to the house, worried now, knowing I was not this bad a cyclist. As I neared the house my mother called to me, her face lined with worry. She was calling my name even louder than before. My playmate, who had reached the house first, ran back to tell me there was an earthquake. When I entered the house the earthquake had stopped. That gave everyone plenty to talk about with the evening wine. In my bed, I could not stop smiling. I had ridden my borrowed bicycle through an Andean earthquake near the mountains that hindered the escape of the clouds.

We left Santiago on an Air Panama flight on the seventeenth of May on our way to Cuba. We had a few hours layover in Peru. A tall couple with curly long hair touching their shoulders, a ribbon around their heads, dark glasses in the shape of tears, jackets, and bell-bottom jeans, carried their guitars as they passed by me and I followed them with my eyes as they walked away talking and laughing. They walked slowly and appeared ready to change directions at any moment, seemingly uncaring about where they were heading or why. That is all I remember about our stay in Peru. That and a policeman in Customs who was vomiting in the bathroom with such force, it appeared he was trying to establish some sort of record. I thought he must be really ill. A few years later I learned that at the Lima airport some Custom employees had a unique way of passing the time. They would count the bottles of Pisco they confiscated from tourists who tried to leave with more bottles than were allowed. This was hard work, sometimes taking most of the night and causing untold upset stomachs.

Following our layover, we boarded a Cubana de Aviación flight to Cuba. It was one of those airplanes where you could smoke and you could peel an apple or an orange with a Swiss Army Knife. No one worried about someone hijacking the airplane with one of the knives or dying of cancer from smoking. It was also impossible to guess who among the passengers would end up slobbering all over his neighbor's shoulder, snoring half the way to the new destination. What a very strange turn my life had taken.

CHAPTER THREE

One day shortly after arriving in Havana, a black Volga, a Russian car, came to pick us up at the hotel. Nestor, the one-eyed chauffeur, was dressed in olive green and had a gun strapped to his belt. He was jovial and very talkative and drove us speedily down the road. We crossed the Almendares River to the neighborhood of Nuevo Vedado where my cousins lived. On the way, Nestor the chauffeur pointed out the zoo and said that we should make the time to see it, that it was a marvelous zoo. I stored that information for a later day. Soon we arrived at the house where my cousins and my aunt Aleida, Che's widow, lived.

Nestor parked the car in front of the house and two of my cousins, Camilo and Ernesto, met us near the driveway. Celita, another cousin, and my aunt Aleida, were inside.

We inspected each other carefully for an instant as we were introduced. We said hello. I felt happy to meet them. They looked like characters from a storybook. Their voices were different as was their way of walking. Ernesto wore his hair close to his head in a buzz cut but with longer bangs in front. He laughed like me and I think we were both feeling shy. Camilo was taller, blonde, and had the same haircut but wore his hair longer than his brother. He was a year older than me. He invited us inside after politely greeting my parents. We took the path through the garden and into the house, where, at the end of a long hallway, my cousin Celita, who was my age, met us. She was very sweet and I liked her right away. Aleidita was the oldest and the most reserved, seeming jealous of sharing her home and perhaps more with her new cousins, but managing to be verbally welcoming. Her mother Aleida gave each of us a kiss. She was a blonde rugged-looking woman with a deep voice, and I could imagine her as someone who would chop wood and carry it home easier than I could think of her as someone who would wait for it to be delivered. As time went on and I got to know and love her, I could never figure out what she and my uncle Che, such different-looking human beings from totally different socioeconomic backgrounds, would talk about when they were alone together. My cousins and I played non-stop that afternoon, running up and down the stairway. The house was pleasant and well lit, painted in bright colors. Later we went out to the street to a corner lot where our cousins taught us new words we would be using on the island. They told me there was one more cousin to meet, the oldest of them all, Hildita. She would arrive later. First we played hide and seek and when we finished Celia said, "Would you like to play *los cogidos*?" Ernesto held my arm. In Argentina, the verb *coger* is a euphemism used to describe making love. I looked at Celia, impressed by so much Caribbean freedom and I blushed at my lack of practice in such matters. I looked at Ernesto who seemed worried by the turn our game was taking—more worried than by the speed in which everything was taking place. I realized that the game being described was the same as the one I called La Mancha, in which the manchado (the stained one), chases everyone attempting to touch them and "stain" them, collecting all he can stain. The game ends when the only player remaining is caught by the rest. God knows that although later in life I loved the game of *cogidos*, that day I was very grateful to have learned a new meaning to that furtive term: its correct meaning on the island. The family had lunch together and by the time dessert came, we had raised quite a raucous telling jokes and sharing anecdotes as if we had known one another all our lives. Some men arrived then, dressed in olive green. Among them were the Acevedo brothers who had been trusted members of my uncle's patrol during the Cuban Revolution. The adults gathered around the table drinking coffee and talking, and we continued to play. I asked where there was a bathroom and Aleida pointed the way. I sat on the toilet and thought about the incredible moments I was living. I felt bad for my cousins because they didn't have a father, but at least they had a house full of people. When I walked out of the bathroom, I was alone in the long hallway that led to the front door. On top of a small entry table there was a black cowboy holster with a gun inside. I extracted the gun very carefully, not wanting to be discovered, and felt its weight, the cold metal against my hand, and the power of the gun. I had never held a handgun. I tied the holster to my waist and went to find Ernesto. I showed him the gun and we agreed to go outside to shoot it, but before we could make our way outside my father and the men dressed in green discovered us and took the gun away. They warned us never to pick up a gun again.

Later they blamed themselves for having left the gun in full view so carelessly. They had been enjoying their coffee and some rum made from sugar cane. They were also getting to know each other and telling jokes.

In the end, besides the new sensation of power I experienced, nothing untoward happened with the gun. But despite the festive energy in the house, one could sense an undercurrent of tragic memories. My cousins took me on a tour of the house that included a visit to my uncle Che's study. It was a large room on the second floor facing the front of the house. It was home to a large library where he liked to spend many hours when he was home. There he read, he contemplated new ideas, and it was a space where he could escape from the darkness of his internal restlessness and from the flies. The study was air-conditioned and the air conditioner served as both insect repellent and climate control. I imagined my heroic uncle sitting behind that desk, and wished with all my heart that I could know him. The room was at once full and empty of his presence. Although the house was a nice house in a section of Havana where families lived comfortably before the Revolution, there was nothing ostentatious about it that announced to the world that a minister of the government lived there. It was ample but simple. It wasn't common to take a home like this for one's own when one had power; the new ruling class preferred the larger houses on the island that had once belonged to the rich. Hildita, my oldest cousin, arrived later in the afternoon. From the time I met her, I could see her as the big sister. She wore a nostalgic look and was very gentle. Many years have passed, many things have changed, and we, the playful dreamers of our childhoods, have grown up. Although we are the same mix of bones and tendons, we have been marked by the fears and the joys we have lived through. But I will never forget the happiness I felt that day. Ernesto and Hildita are parts of me that roam the world, cousins whom I loved and will love as if we were part of the same pack of animals. Hildita was uncle Che's first child and my grandfather's first granddaughter. She was born from my uncle's relationship with Hilda, a Peruvian woman of strong character with whom he shared a passionate but brief affair in the days when much of his time was spent traveling and developing the quixotic spirit that would one day define him. Hilda visited him in jail in Mexico where Che spent a few days in a cell adjoining the one to members of the 26 de Julio Movement that housed

Fidel Castro and his men before he sailed to Cuba on the yacht *Granma*. After the Revolution, when Che ascended to power, he reunited with Hildita and her mother in Havana. Hildita, who had been born in Mexico of an Argentinian father and a Peruvian mother, had arrived on this island to forge yet another Latin American identity. It would become her cross. Uncle Che arrived in Havana already involved in a romantic and military relationship with Aleida, and shortly after their arrival there, they married. Although Hilda was well respected in Havana, she had no clear role there and the situation was uncomfortable. When she was a child, Hildita bounced back and forth between living with her mother and living with her father. Those of us who knew her agreed that her warmth, her courage to confront what she deemed wrong, and her sense of loyalty had been inherited from her father. She could be a great deal of fun, yet be very melancholy. She deeply felt the absence of the father she adored.

Chapter Four

Argentina

My mother María Elena was twenty-four years old when I was born. She was the only child of an Uruguayan ship-welder from the port city of Mar de Plata and a woman from Burgos, Spain, who was a perfect housewife until her death at age ninety. My mother was born, lived, and went to school in San Telmo, the birthplace of the Tango. It was a place infused with the trappings and myth that accompany that dance, much like the tradition of the blues in Mississippi or of jazz in New Orleans; an enclave of stories of men's prowess and famous street fights.

San Telmo begins very near the historical center of Buenos Aires, the national library, and the grave of the designer of the flag, and ends bordering the neighborhood of La Boca. Initially inhabited by Genoese immigrants who left behind a legacy of quaint and colorful houses, La Boca is invaded on the weekends by a species very much in vogue today of half man-half scream, a blending of man and soccer; of kicks, punches, and one-liter bottles of beer. The neighborhood consisted of large two- and three-story houses with a central patio. When the neighborhood was visited twice with lethal violence by yellow fever, the wealthier families abandoned the area and moved to the north of the city. Then the area became the home of a population of freed black slaves until in 1790 most of them died during an epidemic of small pox. Misfortune and extremism are engraved in the history of San Telmo.

Later, these homes were inhabited by workers who came together to share the large spaces much like the *conventillos* or *corrales* of Madrid, and the *solares* of Havana. The *conventillo* was not so much a structure as a way of life. From there came the interminable tango under the streetlight, the pimp, the prostitute, the power of cheap wine, and gin. Troilo and Gardel played their music there. When she was sixteen, my mother was of average height but appeared taller because she was very thin. She carried herself gracefully and her features had a natural refinement. She had an easy but nervous smile, and her straight hair fell loosely on her shoulders.

My mother wanted to stand out, to leave her humble beginnings behind, that mixture of working class and peasant qualities that were her heritage, even if doing so meant she would sacrifice the typically healthy semblance and easy manner that was such an endearing quality in her ancestry. Feeling the call to be an artist but not yet sure what form that art would take, she dreamt of being a poet, a writer, perhaps an actress—which would have suited her histrionic qualities. She looked at life through pretentious eyes, a dubious and unintended gift from parents who had long yearned to have a child and overprotected her accordingly.

She felt haunted by that overprotection, afraid of her own desires, daunted by the enormous obstacles that awaited her in her attempt to overcome the circumstances of her birth. She was apprehensive when she let herself believe that her wishes would come true, for what would life be like when she said goodbye to the morés and complexes with which the working class keeps itself content so long as there is work to be done and bread to serve for dinner?

My paternal grandparents left Castilla-León, Spain, to make a life in Argentina. By the time my mother María Elena was born, she had a myriad of relatives in Argentina, including cousins her same age, and one in particular with whom she plotted her escape from what she perceived to be her drab surroundings. They were children that wanted to use their hands and shoulders in ways other than as the main source of their sustenance, heretics who dared to defy thousands of years of genetic memory. My mother wanted to leave behind the sweat, the blisters on the hands, the cold, and the aching bones. She sought to be respected as a writer or an actor. Money and comfort were secondary to her.

When she was growing up, María Elena was never allowed by my grandmother to make a bed or lift a finger to help her with housework. My mother watched her mother work from morning to night, her duties leaving her little time to attend to my grandfather, an introverted man who didn't enjoy conversation once he got home from work. Only the hot meal and wine that awaited him interested him, and he consumed both with a dose of ill humor. Without any chores to do, my mother was free to concentrate on her studies. She was a very good student, sharp witted, a good conversationalist who liked to tell jokes whenever she could. Her humor was dark and she was not above telling jokes at the expense of others. Despite her seeming extrovert tendencies, my mother carried a shadow inside her much larger and darker than any she could project onto a sidewalk on the sunniest of days.

During her late adolescence, my mother wrote a few verses but did not achieve the success she wanted as a poet. When she finished high school she went to the university to become a journalist. She wanted to channel her literary impulses into a profitable and honorable profession. Soon after starting her studies, she met the man she would marry. My father Juan Martín was twenty years old when he married my mother. He was four years younger than her. He was the son of a man who almost became an engineer, Ernesto Guevara, an ingenuous and colorful representative of the Argentinian middle class who liked to brag that he was an eleventh-generation Argentinian when he frequented social events, where he aspired to be and usually managed to become the center of attention. He also liked to boast that there had never been a Guevara who was a coward, a cuckold, or a homosexual.

My father's mother died young, tormented by pain from an advanced cancer. She was an uncommon woman for her time, one that possessed an audacity that was rarely found in men or women of her era. My grandmother was a young rebel daughter of rich American landowners who eloped with my grandfather to live a life of adventure in a fugitive marriage, with a man her family disapproved of. Her name was Celia de la Serna Llosa, and she was a refined and rich young woman, educated in the best Catholic schools. Her family did not want her to become the wife of a man they found boastful, roguish, and whose fortune did not equal theirs. But grandmother Celia had fallen in love, and finding herself pregnant, she ran away with my grandfather despite her family's vehement objections. She took with her the secret of the child she carried. After their marriage, my grandparents went to live in the north country of Argentina where even today a young woman accustomed to city life would find it hard to feel safe and would probably sleep at night with one eye open.

They bought a sizeable parcel of land to grow maté grass, a traditional Argentinian infusion also used in bordering countries and curiously, also in Syria and Lebanon. Their distance from home ensured that no one they knew would ask impertinent questions about her expanding girth. My grandparents purchased an enormous house in the middle of that land nearby to where the devil had lost his poncho (a Gaucho expression that indicates a faraway place) in the province of Misiones. The Jesuits were the first European settlers of that area and they fought mightily to prevail over the inclement environment. The house was often full of the animals and insects that inhabit that area, generous in variety and size. Outside the house, it was not unusual to see harpy eagles and juagaretés, a type of jaguar. There were also a great variety of reptiles that sometimes found their way inside the house. It was a part of the world where each little creature could eat its fill and develop its muscles in the unlimited space that surrounded it. A mosquito from Misiones would have been a useful ally in conventional aerial combat. But there was another species much more dangerous than the animals, the insects, and the isolation: the owners of bordering maté fields. These men paid their workers with tokens. The workers were able to spend the tokens in the owners' stores on food, and occasionally, on large quantities of distilled spirits. My grandparents, romantic sympathizers of the French Revolution and the rights of men, paid their workers in cash. They paid them a fair wage, as they did not espouse the vulgar communist idea of sharing everything equally. My grandparents espoused a reasonable solidarity, let's say. Still, their actions constituted a threat to the status quo and fanned the fear of contagion. That fear manifested itself as threats from some of their neighbors. My grandmother Celia was forced not only to sleep with one eye open but also with a double-barreled shotgun next to her bed. And she was an excellent shot. Even so, none of their misadventures were able to taint the memories my grandmother treasured from those days in the country. The maté grass business was no doubt doomed to fail, but my grandparents abandoned their life in the country before the fact, when their firstborn made his appearance in Rosario in precarious health.

They named him Ernesto like his father. The world would come to know him as Che. Their son fought hard in that space between the life that awaited him and the nebulous prelude from which he had come. For fifteen long days, he fought while his parents watched over him, with their hearts in their throats, fearing each breath would be his last. No one will ever know how his parents would have loved him had it not been for this experience that brought forth every hue in the color of parental love. Nor can we guess what the spoiled child's character might have been like had it not been tested in that early battle in which life forced him to make a choice, having no criteria to evaluate his options and few weapons with which to engage in combat. What is certain is that the love that was sealed among the three of them during that time of crisis was intensely felt throughout their lives by all of them. Much more is known about the love between Che and his mother. I have to say that his father loved him extraordinarily, but unfortunately, his father had no breasts. In total, five children were born of their union: my father, Juan Martín, the youngest, was conceived when my grandparents had already spent every drop of desire of parenting even cats.

Completely mesmerized by her firstborn, my grandmother didn't pay much attention to any of her younger children, Roberto, Celia, Ana María, or, of course, my father. By the time my father was born, his brothers and sisters were grown. The oldest, Che, was fifteen years older than he, and the youngest, a sister, twelve years older. Because of that age difference, my father did not grow up playing with his brothers and sisters, but instead spent his time playing with the children in his neighborhood as if he had been born an only child. It was Che who took care of him and played with him, showering him with a great deal of affection. This created a deep bond between them.

Because family time at home was limited by his parent's work schedule and his sibling's studies, my father loved to go to the Guevara country house, San Irineo de Portela. In Portela, the Guevara Lynch family liked to get together far away from the noise and activity of the city, and my father could enjoy feeling part of the daily life of his family and basking in the company of his many cousins, aunts, and uncles. In Portela, my father learned the importance of family and became part of the Guevara Lynch clan.

It was in Portela where my father heard the stories of Che's forays into the surrounding forests beginning at the age of three or four. Che would be gone for several days and nights and no one would try to find him. Everyone trusted his ability to come back safely, and he always did. He had become like a little god to his family long before he became a bigger god to the world.

As my father came of age, he experienced many changes. The family began to disperse. His brothers and sisters moved away after their marriages or left to pursue a career, or in Che's case, eventually to help forge a revolution. Also during those years, the family fortune dwindled. The Guevaras continued to belong to an exclusive group of founding families, but now they had to budget their money. They let their servants go, both in their house in the city and in Portela, keeping only one Bolivian maid to help my grandmother with household chores.

They continued to belong to a country club that my grandfather had helped found many years before, where my father Juan Martín played sports. He didn't share the lifestyle of its members. He grew up in a sophisticated bourgeois atmosphere, but his pants couldn't be replaced every time he wore the knees out playing soccer or rugby.

Daily life was otherwise unchanged. Every morning at breakfast there was a review of international news frequently followed by animated discussions about literature and art. Conversations often revolved around the family's solidarity with relatives who were having financial difficulties, the plight of needy children in the neighborhood, the fate of political exiles, and, of course, politics in general. When my father met my mother at the university, they embarked on a long courtship fueled by a strong physical attraction and a mutual interest and militancy in leftist politics. Those were convulsive years in Latin America, and it was common to find young people who felt called to collaborate towards forging a better world. They wanted to challenge the status quo and bring to new generations a planet where justice and peace reigned. Not all agreed on the best way to proceed, and of course, there were those who sought to change the world through violence. Looking back, I can't imagine what drew my parents to each other besides hormones and leftist politics. They were both easy on the eyes, both confused young people who were searching for a better life, both following their own uncertain path. Both were incredibly self-absorbed and uninterested in anything but themselves and their ideas.

Chapter Five

I was born in Buenos Aires, Argentina in May of 1963. The fall in those years marked the beginning of school. Leaves fell and the cold humid weather made its presence felt, invading homes that had not yet readied their stoves or stocked up on fuel.

My arrival coincided with the three-month anniversary of my parents' marriage. They married because I had been conceived six months before. They had been as unprepared for me as some had been for the fall weather. I think if I could recover a gestational memory, I would remember the two months before their wedding as a time of colossal anxiety, long silences, and a burning desire to get the pregnancy over with.

My parents once told me that I was a much-wanted child, after the eighth month of my mother's pregnancy. My paternal grandfather Ernesto gave my parents an apartment as a wedding present. The apartment was located in a beautiful neighborhood of Buenos Aires called Belgrano, where even now after the hard economic times the city has suffered, one can enjoy its unspoiled beauty. People played soccer in the plazas of Belgrano filling them with color and the smell of leather—leather from the soccer balls bearing that scent so characteristic of the animals, a scent that always lingers in my memory.

Not long after my birth my father bought a small but very popular bookstore on Corrientes Street where many of the bookstores and theaters in Buenos Aires are located. The bookstore was next door to my grandfather Ernesto's office and its shelves held books written by some of our relatives. Books like Benito Lynch's *Raquela* and his best-known work *El Inglés de los Guesos*. Benito stopped writing abruptly and took the secret of why he had done so to his grave.

The bookstore also carried books by my grandmother's relative, the Peruvian author Mario Vargas Llosa, who is considered as important as Gabriel García Márquez.

The bookstore was frequented by interesting and colorful characters, many of them friends of my parents who were more interested in social interaction and literary conversation than in purchasing books. La Pulga, as the bookstore was called, was best known as Che's brother's bookstore. The bookstore became a place where friends gathered to discuss politics and the ideologies that were popular at the time. These things were discussed in low voices for although the sixties in Argentina shone with the promise of possibility, they also harbored much darkness, fear, and despair.

In addition to books, my parents sold new and used long-playing vinyl records that were displayed in the store windows where passers-by would stop to browse their covers. Their prominence helped distract passers-by from the activity inside the store. Later in my life I stayed in touch with very good friends of my parents from that era, friends who frequented their bookstore, and they shared with me the pleasure they experienced there. They spoke of the late nights full of passionate discussions and of how they took turns holding me until I fell asleep and how they put me to bed in a small crib away from the din of the conversation, the lights, and the cigarette smoke. It was not unusual for the bookstores on Corrientes Street to stay open until three or four in the morning on weekends, but I was put to bed long before unless I was having trouble sleeping. Sleeplessness has plagued me throughout my life. Sometimes now, right before sleep finally overtakes me, I feel as if I can smell the pipe smoke from my parents' friend Marcos's pipe, as I did when I lay in his arms back in those days, awake but content, my ears full of the sounds of voices engaged in animated conversation. My parents owned the bookstore until I was three years old, but the scent of used books, the classical music in the background, and the passionate conversations between my parents and their friends remain locked in my sense memory. Perhaps the pleasure I find in reading had its beginning on Corrientes street, in my parents' small bookstore that my grandfather helped them buy.

I think my mother loved that bookstore most of all. Her relationship with books was intense and genuine, because the love of words coursed through her veins. Her mother's reminiscences of Spain, the old sayings that her mother used to teach moral lessons, the centuries-old popular music she sang, were the closest thing to literature my mother had known as a child; her first exposure to the transformational power of words. Her ancestors had been men who knew that everything could be transformed with the sound of their tools. But she could feel a vibration that ran through her being when she read, or heard the cadence of a verse.

When I was two years old we moved from Belgrano to a new neighborhood, Olivos. Olivos was a residential area of one- and two-story houses with colorful gardens, north of greater

Buenos Aires. My grandfather Ernesto, having made the ostentatious gesture of gifting my parents with their apartment, asked them to give it back so he could pay off debts he incurred in one of his businesses. The ability my grandfather Ernesto possessed to get involved in businesses that were doomed to fail was uncanny. He had an innate talent for chancing upon such businesses. From the time he married my grandmother, he was either managing or participating in businesses that invariably fell short of success.

I don't remember my paternal grandmother Celia. She died when I was a very little boy. My first outing in this life, the first time that I left my home, was to go visit her in prison where she had been incarcerated upon returning to Argentina after traveling in Europe. She had visited Prague, Paris, and several Italian cities, reentering Argentina through Uruguay. Guards awaited her at the border crossing between Uruguay and Argentina. She was apprehended for transporting subversive literary material, for her support of the Cuban Revolution, and for her visits to and support of her son Che, a commandant of said revolution. Most of all she was arrested because at that time in Argentina there was no tolerance for difference and the different had to spend time behind bars. The books in question like *The Agrarian Reform in Uruguay*, speeches by Fidel Castro, and works by John Williams Cooke and Framini, two leftist Peronistas, represented more danger than *The Red and Black* by Stendhal; enough difference to cause a genteel woman to be roughly apprehended. During my visit to her jail cell, she held me in her arms and whispered tenderly in my ear. Perhaps the iron bars had softened her or perhaps her age had, although I don't entirely discount the possibility that I was a charming baby. She wrote about that visit in a letter to my uncle Che. In that letter she tells Che that my father and his baby boy visited her and she spoke of me with tenderness. Che, who was always particularly fond of my father, responded in kind. The truth is that my parents had to visit my grandmother in jail and they wanted to introduce me to her and in doing so show her that the future was already among them. There is historical proof of the fact that I was welcome in the loving correspondence between my uncle Che and his mother. Surprisingly, my grandmother Celia and my mother forged a strong friendship. Even today one of the few things that can rouse my mother is an insult or a slight to my grandmother Celia. They visited one another frequently, and my mother was often by her side during the last days of her life.

People who knew her say that my grandmother was an exceptional woman. She was daring and elegant in the extreme. In the society laden with prejudices within which she moved, she stood out like a rare brightly-plumed bird among pigeons. She sat astride her horse instead of sidesaddle like the ladies of her time. She was one of the first women to smoke and to cut her hair in a short bob. She gave her political opinion in every gathering and faced danger with amazing aplomb. She was an excellent marksman and Bridge player. It is said that her death was very painful due to the cancer that consumed her. She was incarcerated twice while ill and she never lost her inner strength. She was eventually released due to the severity of her illness. Those who witnessed her pain say they never heard her complain. Others describe my grandmother as a dour woman, rigorously harsh and insensitive. They believe that Che's quarrelsome character was her legacy to him. I disagree. I believe that his father had just as much influence in shaping his character as his mother did. Her death at age fifty-six was a great blow to Che, not only because she died so young, but because he fervently yearned to see her one last time and couldn't, and because he had learned that she never received the heart-felt letter he wrote her with so much love, saying good-bye.

CHAPTER SIX

My childhood years passed without any major upheavals, except for the excessive number of times that we moved. In ten years, we moved five times. My friends remained the same because I was able to stay in the same school despite the frequent moves. I attended the Colegio Nacional Number Seventeen, Don José de San Martín, named after the national hero of the independence of Chile, Argentina, and Peru.

When I was two years old my brother Pablo was born, and when I was five, my sister Ana followed, a pearl that brought much grace to our family. By then my maternal grandparents, Elena and Miguel, had moved in with us.

My grandmother Elena loved my father like a son. She washed and ironed his clothes and fed him as if he'd never been fed, even though he was from a good family and she was only a Castilian peasant. My grandmother fed us breakfast every morning, washed clothes, cooked our food, and put us to bed at night. Perhaps for all those reasons there may have been little

Shadow of a Myth

resistance to my grandparents' invasion of our home. My parents were inconvenienced, but my grandparents' moving in with us was like a small aftershock compared to the earthquake of my birth a few years earlier.

Perhaps my father would have become a very strong man had it not been for my maternal grandparents' intrusion in our lives. My father, like his brother Che, harbored the idea that giving in to temptation weakens one's character. They shared a belief that the less a man enjoys food, the less he laughs, and the less he indulges himself, the stronger his character becomes. My grandmother's cooking proved to be too much of a temptation for my father to resist.

For us children, having our grandparents in our home was a wonderful experience, although perhaps the patron saint of marriage did not feel the same way.

The seven of us, siblings, parents, and grandparents, lived together with my stuffed bear. I had been given Cocó for my birthday when I was three months old. Until I was five he was my confidant. He was the eighth member of the household. Frequently I felt inadequate and I would talk about my feelings with Cocó. I confided in him how it felt not to be gifted in sports and to be shy. Cocó knows more about my world than I will ever imagine. After having been thrown on the roof, burned, kicked, and beheaded in fits of anger and then re-stitched, Cocó now rests in my dresser drawer along with my most valuable documents.

Back then my shyness was extreme. When someone looked my way, my toes curled, and possibly other things did, too. My hands would tense and I almost managed to make my face invisible. I wished the moment of observation, a moment that felt uncomfortable and eternal, would end quickly.

Back in those days I was under the impression that my temperament made it difficult for people to love me. Even now I find it hard to look at pictures of myself when I was little.

There was a bright spot during those years, when I discovered that I was able to express myself through my drawings. Almost simultaneously, my grandfather Miguel and my aunt Celia, my uncle Che's sister, discovered my talent. At least this gift of art gave me a small sense of worth.

My aunt Celia encouraged me to draw. She was an architect, a lover of art, who took aesthetics very seriously. She taught me some drawing technique and entered me in a contest. I drew a ship in a harbor with a difficult three-quarter perspective and drew it well, and though the drawing is not exhibited in the Louvre and is not part of anyone's private collection, it was very important to me. I earned an award as an artist and my aunt Celia was proud of my achievement. A close relationship developed between us. It is a relationship that has benefited me more than any other family relationship, because it connected me with an extraordinary human being, my aunt Celia, and with art.

I spent many afternoons drawing and attempting to paint what I drew. I enjoyed seeing what I had imagined take form. It took years to perfect my dinosaur and my horse, and eventually my drawings became populated with men sitting at bars, alone or with women with lit cigarettes in their hands, always with placid expressions. They were my last drawings, drawn to pass the time and tame the beast that grew in me, a beast that would someday demand much more potent and much less edifying tranquilizers.

I was drawn to solitude in part because of my shyness. Nevertheless I truly wished to be like Ricardo Bochini, the star of my favorite soccer team. It is possible that I wanted the glory of success, but not when I considered that to attain that glory would require me to jump like someone possessed, and hug everyone with whom I had nothing in common but the color of our shorts and t-shirts. That's another thing, the shorts; I didn't feel very comfortable with the ankles given to me by nature. There were no socks tight enough to adhere to such skinny bones.

In addition to Cocó, I had very good friends. My best friend was Juan Martín. He had bangs like me and was just as skinny. We were inseparable. One summer we went to visit the farm where his grandfather was the overseer. I went without my mother. I lost a tooth while visiting the farm. It was our custom in the city that when a child lost a tooth, Little Mouse Pérez left money under his or her pillow. The amount was proportional to the parents' financial situation, and since he was so considerate, he was welcome in almost all the homes in Argentina. I was used to a Little Mouse Pérez that was quite generous, but when I woke up to find a ten-dollar bill under my pillow, I felt very happy!

Juan Martín and I spent long lazy days having fun together playing games, running, and drinking in every experience.

Juan Martín's uncle hired the men who worked the farm and was in charge of them. One day he ordered some workers to make us an asado, a delicious Argentinian roast. We were to watch a complete asado being prepared, from beginning to end.

The ritual begins when the barbecue oven is heated with the charcoal, and the ribs, chorizos, intestines, flank, and any fresh meat, is placed on the grill. The workers group around the grill seated on tree trunks, stones, or stools that in the old days were made from the bones of the cow. A cow's head with the horns turned sideways can be a comfortable seat for a tired worker on the endless plains.

Every day the sound of a musical triangle called the workers to their lunch, but one day they called us at the very beginning of the day. A worker brought out a lamb. He hung it from a tree, and without an explanation, as we were used to when in our classroom, he sank his knife into the side of the lamb's throat. He opened it wide, cutting in a straight line—a hole Moses himself could have crossed had he not been in such a hurry to part the waters. The animal began bleating in a concert of protest, very long and loud bleating. It was an unmistakable sound of suffering. The lamb wouldn't stop screaming and bleeding. I was petrified. In time I was able to move, and walked a few yards away from the spectacle. This was my first close encounter with violence and brutality and my first collusion with it, as a short time later I enjoyed my herb-roasted leg of lamb along with the workers.

I have never minded the taste of meat, but since that day I abhor being present at the death of any animal caused directly by the hand of man, be it by blows, thumps, kicks, garrotes, or knives. I lament any death caused by violence or abuse, and most of all I lament the total absence of scruples of the man that never asks himself if he could be wrong. Today I reflect on that fact. Back then I was in shock and to this day the bleating of a lamb as it is being beheaded brings back jumbled memories of a hardened old cowhand who treated us like little men, and a small helpless animal that had no wish to give up its life to be consumed by us.

Since that day I know that no matter what impression the murderous knife leaves in me, once the smell of the meat on the grill or in the oven invades my nasal passages, I have enough imagination to forget the incident and exchange my grief and my doubt for a huge appetite and the ability to satisfy it.

We swam in the pool every day during our stay at the ranch, until one afternoon my mother and Juan Martín's mother suddenly appeared. I had forgotten that I belonged to another space, to a different world and a different family. My mother and Juan Martín's mother put on their bathing suits, enjoyed an afternoon in the sun, and a few hours later told us it was time to go home.

I became angry and made a scene that embarrassed my mother. The time had come to leave. We knew the time was coming but it felt as far away as the day we would grow old. My mother had to sit by my side and convince me, not without some tenderness, that we had to let Juan Martín's grandfather rest. I thought: *You'll see mom, you'll see how Juan Martín's grandfather will say: "No one is taking these children away."* I was convinced of it. He had shown us so much respect!

I couldn't have been more wrong. I still recall the speed with which my friend's grandfather bid us good-bye, with a kiss to each of our foreheads. He said:

"Come on kids, don't upset your mothers. Go!"

The poor old man was up to his ears with our company, but he had treated us so well! During the drive home I told my mother about the wonderful present from Little Mouse Pérez as if announcing that from that day on I would not accept anything less than the same amount of money for subsequent lost teeth. *If I have to leave I might as well take with me a lasting gift*, I thought.

I don't remember which tooth I lost next or how much money El Ratoncito Perez brought me. Obviously it wasn't even close to what I received at the farm since I still remember those ten dollars as a supreme gift.

Chapter Seven

We had our very own fields at Portela. They weren't inhabited by cowhands, nor was the old man with the whip, Juan Martín's grandfather, in residence there. Our farm was the place where all the cousins met sometime during the year. It was there that like my uncle Che, I forged a deep friendship with my cousins, in particular with my cousins Juan and his sister Rosario. Juan and Rosario lived in northern Argentina. Their parents were architects and had projects that demanded their presence in the area.

Every time we made the trip to the countryside my father would ready our truck and help my mother climb up to her seat. My father's face, when he turned on the ignition and began the ride to Irineo de Portela, was the picture of happiness. Irineo de Portela had been the grand home of my great grandmother, Ana Lynch. My mother enjoyed everything that made my father happy, but she did not enjoy the country with its insects, horses, cows, reptiles, trees, and trails. But none of that mattered in the face of being able to allow her husband to enjoy himself and she made sure never to share her discomfort. I was ecstatic when we arrived. I would jump from the truck and run to see which bed would be mine during our stay. The beds were old with antique metal headboards and beautiful because of their age. The first of the cousins to arrive would get the best bed. It never occurred to me to unpack my bags. As soon as I was satisfied with my choice of bed, I took off like a shot running as fast as I could—as if pursued by a lightning bolt, to greet my cousins. The café con leche (coffee with milk) of the house in Portela is still the measure my brain uses to compare all the café con leches every morning. Not only was the flavor unforgettable because it was excellent, but in the kitchen, the huge coffee-maker blowing steam had a prominent position and the aroma filled the air in that special way that seems to be typical of old country homes. We feasted on bread and butter, and coffee.

When I first got to know Portela, it was a mansion surrounded by a few acres. Destined for enjoying lazy days, for family reunions, there were still a few caretakers and cowhands in residence. In its heyday it had been a vast farm, prime land inside the city limits of Buenos Aires, and extremely valuable.

Not only had my grandfather Ernesto been somewhat careless with the businesses he started, but other relatives had also been. They sold parcels of Portela to cover their losses. Other relatives sold parcels for a different reason. They had done so well that they had no interest in caring for a land that needed so much tending, along with animals and structures. My father was one who eventually sold his share of that rich land. The history of that land was told to the children who treasured their time in its midst, and that history bonded them to one another and to the land. My paternal great grandmother, Ana Lynch Ortiz, after whom Portela had been originally named, was married to Roberto Guevara Castro. Ana and Roberto were born in California, where their parents had gone in search of adventure. My grandmother Ana Lynch Ortiz married Roberto Guevara Castro. They were both born in California, two families that became Guevara Lynch when several of Roberto's brothers married several of Ana's sisters. Due to a variety of reasons related to both politics and adventure, both families were exiled in Chile after a dictator named Rosas confiscated their lands in neighboring Mendoza, along with the lands of future Argentinian democrats like Mitre Alberdi and Sarmiento.

One afternoon at the beginning of the year 1848, Lieutenant Lynch and the brothers Guevara, along with Sarmiento, were discussing the political climate of the times, when their friend José Carreas approached them with the news that fabulous amounts of gold had been discovered in California. All felt seduced by the vile ore except Sarmiento, who was an already mature and wise man and who advised them that by the time they arrived in California, the gold would be gone. Youth seldom listens to the elders' wisdom and so weeks later, having acquired a brig with two sails, the future millionaires embarked towards San Francisco, where they arrived in the winter of that year. Upon their arrival they found a city in indescribable chaos. The brothers and their friends managed to sell their brig after many failed attempts. The Guevaras headed for Sacramento and the promised land of gold. Lynch decided to stay in San Francisco, having married Eloisa Ortiz. Lynch opened a saloon called Pleasures of California and did quite well with his new venture. Not so his friends, who were forced to return to San Francisco, exhausted and poorer. Lynch gave them jobs in the saloon and there they met Guillermo Castro, an aristocrat from the city, who was married to the granddaughter of Peralta, the former Viceroy of New Spain, now Mexico, who even owned the Grand Canyon at that time.

When General Urquiza deposed Rosas, the Guevaras returned to Argentina. Lynch returned a few years later with his large family of seventeen children and a considerable fortune.

Both families, now tied by blood, were given back their lands in Argentina. In reality, those lands did not belong to either family but to the aborigines that grew up in that land of volcanoes and plains, the Mapuches, who, when they had to abandon their animals and homes, had no brig to embark on in a voyage to the American West, nor the perspicacity to think of opening a saloon dedicated to pleasure. I am certain that my great-great-grandparents were gold seekers. They rode through the American West looking for that ever-precious metal. They had children there, many children, as was the custom of the time, and several of the Guevara brothers married Lynch sisters. The families were thrilled to be able to keep their Argentinian identity intact despite the distance and time for sentimental and for social-status reasons. Despite the distance, they had preserved the bloodlines of founding families of Argentina, families who could deed few things to Che, or to any creature, on the subject of the respect of human rights, the equality of race, or of class. But on the subject of adventure, of the cellular sensation of alertness that translates into our flight-or-fight response they had much they could contribute. My grandfather kept Santa Ana once his mother died. There, where I would later spend some of the happiest days of my childhood in Argentina, he had lived wonderful days with his siblings, as had his own father. That is why that land, already reduced to a smaller hedonistic space, continued to provide joy and happiness to a family who regardless of its blessings or its tragedies has always approached life as if it were a wild horse to be tamed. My father loved that house so much that he never set limits on anything we wanted to do during our stay there. It was in Portela that he taught me how to ride a horse, how to mount it from the left side, and how to use the reins to control it. He put me on a horse called El Doradillo, The Golden One, and I rode him often.

One terrible day El Doradillo was hit by a train and his guts had spilled out. His stomach was sewn back up but he was never able to work again. He was put out to pasture and spent his life breeding until the day he died. His only duty was to be ready at the sound of my dad's whistle, and he responded happily. Perhaps El Doradillo thought that the afternoon of the train had not been so disastrous and that he had healed for the purpose of living life galloping in the sun without a saddle, or listening for the sound of my father's whistle announcing that several lumps of sugar awaited him.

I have always loved and respected horses almost more than dogs. I love them for their goodness and respect them for the centuries of service to man both in his work and at times of war. But perhaps the reason I love them so is because when I see a horse, I remember my father, happy to spend time with me.

It was in Portela that my father taught me to shoot with a twenty-two-caliber rifle. Even though I was an arrant pacifist, I remember that time with my father as a very special time. We were riding our horses under eucalyptus trees near the pigpens, when he slid his rifle out of its scabbard and said: "Here, shoot." I was filled with a marvelous sensation that no matter how hard I tried I could not turn into anything negative despite the displeasure that the idea of guns normally filled me with. Shooting with my father was like enjoying an asado after the beheading of a lamb. Above all, my father taught me to enjoy the simple pleasure of riding through the countryside. Once he took me to an old abandoned dovecote that was falling apart due to its age. It was there that he told me the story of Portela in a fleeting moment of closeness between us.

My uncle Che had loved spending time on the farm. He had forged a loving relationship with his grandmother Ana and his paternal aunt Beatriz who loved him like a son. In those fields even my grandmother Celia was happy. Her family had rejected her for a time after she married my grandfather and she had been unable to enjoy the Echague farm, a farm that meant as much to the La Serna family as Portela did to the Guevaras. That is why Che, who was extremely close to his mother, formed such a close bond with the Guevara troop that went to Portela to rest, in the house of the fun grandmother from California. During one of our times at Portela when lots of cousins and aunts and uncles were in residence, a room full of children who weren't ready to fall asleep gathered to tell each other jokes and stories. During one of those gatherings, I found out that all my cousins were Catholic, or at least had been baptized Catholic. I learned they had two names because of the Church, and I felt unique because I didn't participate in this Church that none respected, which was obvious from their conversation in the darkness of our room.

I felt proud not to be like them, to believe in what I am, and never to have been educated in that double standard of religion, shortly before succumbing in pieces to another temple of the double standard, the moral of communism. My cousins talked to me all the next day about the devil and the angels, and how they believed none of it. I couldn't understand why they were so caught up in something they didn't believe in.

My brother, my sister, and I only had one name and my head, unless sprinkled upon by a Buenos Aires rain, was never sprinkled by anything that was not the hot-water faucet of the small bathtub of our home. I was a heretic, an infidel: a wanderer between the heavens and earth.

Once a classmate invited me to attend a first communion and I went without knowing what it was. My parents told me it was a religious feast and that they would pick me up after it was over. It was my friend Bonafide's First Communion. He was named after a famous brand of Argentinian candy. At the reception I had my first ever taste of beer. I must have been eight or nine years old. I was still dizzy when it came time for my parents to pick me up. Alcohol and faith: a Revolution without Christ awaited me.

CHAPTER EIGHT

In 1973, after three years under a military government, my country returned to democracy. The back and forth between civil and military rule has been very common in Argentinian society.

Perón, the Nationalist leader of Argentina in the twentieth century, had been deposed. In 1955, he was defeated during a revolution led by his opposition in the army and by an oligarchy of cattle barons. The revolution was called the Revolución Libertadora (the Liberating Revolution). Perón ran away like a bat out of hell, leaving his supporters behind to die in the Plaza de Mayo, across from the house of government. His fleeing was congruent with his having taken power and not wanting to step down, as it would be contradictory that someone who wants to occupy the highest seat of power until their biological end, would be willing to die in a mere skirmish.

Argentina was living moments of great social conflict. Many young people became militants in various leftist parties that demanded major changes in the country. The influence of the

Cuban Revolution and its resistance to its powerful northern neighbor despite its proximity was as undeniable as the influence of a not-disinterested world-power despite its geographical distance. Besides the traditional parties like the Communist Party, the Socialist Party, and other smaller parties that called for a pacifist and democratic solution to social problems, there were other more radical parties and groups that called for change through violence and armed combat. Some were Marxists, others Marxist-Leninists, or Trotskians. The majority were Peronists, followers of Perón. The degree of violence depended on which organization was involved.

The Marxist parties wanted to take power and espoused a complete transformation of Argentinian society. The Nationalists wanted power but they espoused no strategy for change. Their goal was the return of Perón, the return of the Third Option, a theory that held that all social classes could coexist harmoniously, including the bourgeoisie and the workers, those that Marxism condemned to an eternal disagreement. As time passed I think that perhaps it would not have been a bad idea to allow that theory to unfold. If it was a peaceful proposition, there wasn't much to lose. It is also true that making a fire out of existing logs is less exhausting than going out to chop wood. Argentina was a time bomb. While the youth, inspired by change, gave the best of itself as well as its worse, Perón prepared his return through one of his supporters, Cámpora, who won the election because Perón was not a candidate. Argentinian money began a habit that later worsened. It became addicted to devaluation. In April of 1973, the decision was made to leave our country. The decision was also made not to tell me and my brother and sister that the leaving would be indefinite.

Chapter Nine

Cuba

The penchant for lying that had always found a place in our home began to show signs of becoming an addiction. Vacation was over. It was time for the fun to come to an end. I wasn't ready to leave the island although I was yearning to see my friends and tell them everything about my time in Havana. I asked my parents when we were going back to Argentina, because my school had already started and I was anxious to rejoin my classmates. They told me that we would stay in Havana for the school year that would begin in September and that soon I would have to don a new uniform, meet new teachers, and learn new rules. When I asked about my friends, they told me not to worry, that I would make lots of new friends. Then my father said: "Now it is time for you to learn to be a good revolutionary."

One day soon after a man came to our suite. My brother, my sister, and I were told that we had to call the man Comrade Onis.

He was from ICAP, Instituto Nacional de Amistad con los Pueblos (National Institute of Friendship with other Countries). He was one of our entourage. He handed us three uniforms: navy shorts, a sky blue shirt, a red beret, and a triangular white-and-blue scarf tied with a red cylinder that served as a knot. It was the uniform of Los Pioneros, the children in whose hands the future of the Cuban Revolution rested.

The first school we attended was next to our hotel, but we were only there for a very short time. That part of the neighborhood was very crowded and had few primary schools. I began my Socialist Primary in 1973 in Orlando Pantoja school, located on Fifteenth and L streets in El Vedado, in the city of Havana.

As a child I liked to play with the hair that fell over my eyes, moving it to the side so it wouldn't impede my vision. I had to stop doing that because I was told that my hair would be cut short. Long hair was not appropriate for a revolutionary. Not appropriate for a true man. The honorable exceptions were the Commandants of the Revolution who despite being the hairiest, were the best revolutionaries, and, of course, the truest men.

Every morning when we arrived at school we had to queue up as we did in Argentina, salute the flag, and sing the National Anthem. There were two new aspects to the start of my school day in my new country. Each day, without fail, the first- through sixth-grade students assembled to a greeting from a disembodied voice coming from an intercom. The forceful voice said: *¡Pioneros por el comunismo!* and we responded, *¡Seremos como el Che!* ("Pioneers for communism! We will be like Che!")

It was a phrase I had to find a way of distancing myself from in order to maintain a semblance of sanity in my life.

"*¡Pioneros por el comunismo!*" the intercom would say to all who in their different vocations might find their way to power and the prestidigitation of politics. But they also said it to those in whom there was not the slightest inclination to dedicate more than that morning routine to matters of ideology, as was my case. And they said it also, of course, to the masses of children who would fall asleep or push the classmate standing in front of them, or who were looking at the cute girl next to them. All would respond:

"¡Seremos como el Che!"

Children from six to twelve years old; what were we supposed to understand? That we would cut our university studies short to travel the world on a motorized bicycle carrying our diaries with us until we found our life's purpose? Well, not exactly. A medical student was absolutely forbidden to leave the country until he graduated and completed five years of social service. Traveling for the simple purpose of seeing the world was reserved for high-ranking officials. So, were they guiding us to voice our dissatisfaction with that which in our opinion was poorly done or that which according to our values was a grave injustice? No! By God, that certainly was not being suggested in the least! Not unless they wanted all of us to end up behind bars, and let us not even imagine a system that would be so cruel!

Then what message were we sending with this mantra we repeated with such intensity in the early hours of the morning? What message was this that had substituted the prayers in the schoolyard of the children who came before us? I asked myself what qualities of my uncle's we should adopt until we were indistinguishable from him. Were we being ordered to triumph in a guerrilla war like the Cuban Revolution? Or perhaps they wanted us to die completely alone and abandoned while forging a revolution in another country like Bolivia. Abandoned by everyone. Or were we perhaps being told to become government ministers with iron wills and the character and the charisma of the Pied Piper of Hamelin?

"*¡Seremos como el Che!*"

I preferred to think we were being invited to be men of great conviction that had little to do with politics; men who loved poetry, who read Proust, Rousseau, Cervantes, Goethe or Sartre, lovers of empiric knowledge attuned to the purpose of life and the soul. But maybe we were being called to become like the bureaucrat ashamed of being bourgeois, to succumb to the excesses of power and to arrive at our inevitable solitary and final destiny? Sandokán leading his tigers of Mompracem in the ultimate battle; the writer of an action novel who, having submerged himself so deeply in its plot, had no choice but to carry out his protagonist's purpose, sacrificing himself and leaving others to write the ending.

I didn't know which of the mythological and legendary qualities attributed to my uncle we should emulate. In any case, inside Che lived Ernesto, the man oblivious to the status that would be conferred upon him. Ernesto, the man who slept on his side, who picked his nose when no one was looking, who felt the gamut of human emotions felt by all humans. A great and small man, a man like all men, with merits and faults, with values and fears; ill and competitive, proud and brave sometimes, cold and ruthless at others. A man who has been flooded with qualities attributed to him by his biographers, who like many biographers present their subjects as men who never needed a handkerchief, or toilet paper.

I started school in Cuba in the fifth grade at the age of ten. The school day started at eight thirty in the morning with several recesses until noon, when all of us Pioneros would go to lunch at another school nearby. After lunch, we played in a huge patio and after recess we went back to our school building for an afternoon session until four twenty in the afternoon, at which time we left for home.

One day on the way home, while being battered by a torrential rain, I found a newborn kitten. I picked him up and took him to the hotel. Although I walked distracted by my thoughts, I saw him because I was looking down. From the time I began to walk, I did so looking down, looking at stones, bugs, and at times simply lost in my thoughts. When I walked I liked to analyze my thoughts, explore each corner of those thoughts, and find a place to plant the seeds of new ideas. Walking looking downward during childhood served two purposes: one, the development of my imagination and two, avoiding being chosen to catch a ball by any sports team. It also kept me out of trouble.

I arrived at the hotel lobby with my drenched kitten, and the elevator operator told me I couldn't take animals upstairs. I started to argue with him at the same moment that a woman I had never seen before entered the elevator. She had an Argentinian accent and she mildly resembled my mother. She said she was a doctor and she was authorized to take the kitten to her room. She got off on my floor. We had moved to the twenty-first floor because the fifteenth floor was carpeted and the combination of the dust trapped by the carpet and the humidity of the island exacerbated my asthma. On the twenty-first floor, there was no carpeting, only marble floors.

The woman told me she and her family had arrived two days before, that she had a son my age and another son who was older. She was from Argentina. She was the mother of the friend who would share many adventures with me throughout my stay in the hotel. She told me that she really was a doctor, a psychiatrist, and that the kitten was too small to survive. She said I should give him milk with a dropper, keep him warm with cotton and give him lots of attention, and perhaps he would live. I looked at my new kitten and thought that little and fragile as he was, he had probably lived and experienced more adventures than he would find on the twenty-first floor of our hotel if he survived. I thanked my new friend and went to our room.

The kitten managed to live through the week, a virtual miracle! When I found him, his eyes hadn't opened yet and he scooted across the sidewalk unable to walk. When the management of the hotel came to tell me the kitten had to leave now that I had saved his life, the kitten looked to be the size of a big cotton ball. Of course, I wasn't inclined to follow anyone's orders, especially now that I had learned I had to be like an uncle who said no injustice should be tolerated.

What I was being asked to do was an absolute injustice, particularly in view of the fact that Cubans, after years of having their food rationed, didn't consider eating cat meat complete madness. The Chinese horoscope considers the year of the cat and the rabbit the same. I was told the flavor of their meat was similar.

In the end, my new friend's mother told me to leave the kitten with her, that the hotel management would not bother her. I did so. It gave me an excuse to frequent Fernando's room more often. Fernando was my age and size, skinny like me, and easily provoked to laughter. Like me, he loved animals. Fernando had been born in Cuba ten years earlier. His father was one of those revolutionaries that like my uncle had liberated Cuba.

His father was a journalist who served with the founder of Prensa Latina, Massetti. Massetti would later take arms joining in a guerrilla movement in the north of Argentina where he succeeded in dying an obscure death. It isn't known if he died of hunger or from the rigors of the jungle. The police and the Argentinian oligarchy gave the uprising very little importance.

The indigenous people in the area, those seen as the oppressed, did not see themselves in that light. They had felt distant from the Spanish conquerors and the landowners who exploited them, from any white man, including these men who asked them to die for a revolution conceived by a German and a

Russian that would deliver them from evil, just as the church and their Jesuit missionaries had tried to do centuries earlier.

Fernando's mother and father instead of going to die in the southern jungles had opted to work on the island in the company of mosquitoes. Palm trees and rum were substantially healthier than the insects of the jungle. They made the right choice.

Later they returned to Argentina, so my friend, despite being Cuban, spoke like an Argentinian. He had an Italian and a Polish surname and outside of the tango and the gaucho, few things are more typical of Argentina. Only Milanese sandwiches, which despite my newfound love of mangoes and shrimp, I couldn't stop yearning for.

My cat lived with my new friend, not in the room that he shared with his older brother, but in his mother's room. She bottle fed him and took care of him and I developed a great deal of affection for her because of the care she gave the little creature. I liked that she kept her word, that what she said was in line with reality. The fusion of word and truth in my life was so rare it had become an endangered species. I perceived words were only respected in the moment the sound was formed and that respect lasted only as long as a conversation.

Each day I was told that I was living in a perfect society because we were all equal. I was told that in the country I came from medicine had to be paid for as well as school, that everything except the air we breathed in Argentina came at a price, which is why most people were very poor and ambled the streets begging for food and work. Even though it had been only a few months since I had left those streets full of beggars and people dying of hunger, I had absolutely no memory of them and felt guilty for missing a country that was so cruel to everyone.

Instead, I remembered that in my country I was only a child equal to all the other children. But in Cuba, even though I was constantly told that we were all equal, as soon as I stepped outside the Hotel Habana Libre, it was obvious that some of us were more equal than others.

The guests of the hotel and the inhabitants of the city were vastly different in their dress. Inside the hotel, the guests wore colorful and stylish clothing. In the city, people wore three or four types of shirts and pants and everyone wore similar shoes. Everyone applied ugly heavy grease to their hair and was perfumed by the same heavy sweet scent. There was an alternative perfume from Bulgaria, but it wasn't always available. The bottle was much nicer than the scent of the perfume, a bottle in the shape of an orthodox byzantine copula made of wood.

The food at our hotel and the food available in the city to the average person were vastly different. The food in the hotel was like the food in Argentina and other capitalist countries. In school we ate a lot of protein, but each Cuban in their home ate just enough protein to preserve their health. All available beverages were healthy, but the war between the system and esthetics was strident and extended to the food's flavor.

Anything that could engender enthusiasm in one's taste buds appeared to be as subversive as chocolate had been in the Catholic Church of the seventeenth century, when it was considered a satanic substance for inciting erotic pleasure. It was open season on the exquisite. Socialism would not tolerate sophistication. Anything that had been related to the bourgeois was extinguished.

All those forbidden products, however, were available in the refrigerators of the revolutionaries: those who had proven themselves worthy. It was easy to understand that those who fought in sierras and mountains could overcome such temptations without succumbing to vice or being corrupted by gluttony. Apparently, those of us who lived at the hotel also possessed those heroic qualities.

Perhaps instead of considering us privileged for having access to such feasts, the people needed to understand that we were a prodigy of sacrifice because we were always being placed in a position of grave risk, facing the abyss of falling prey to our weaknesses while in addition having to do homework. Every day we engaged in combat with the corruption of the soul, every time we sat in front of our lunch or dinner, faced with plates full of fish soaked in French sauces or fruit sauces and delicious meats prepared by chefs. We were demonstrating our loyalty, our resistance to small bourgeois vices.

When we came home from school and went swimming in the pool, the cooks prepared ham-and-cheese sandwiches and Paneque served us poolside on tables next to the diving board. Maybe our greatest show of strength was when we ordered room service and cousins and friends shared soft-boiled eggs and French fries—later used to play war with, in the long hotel hallways: we threw food at each other but preferred the eggs because they stayed encrusted to the walls and doors; they were hen's eggs, pre-chickens. The same prized delicacies outside the hotel, in the city, outside our center of constant sacrifice, were named "lifesavers" for their role in helping the people survive hunger during the tough days of the Revolution.

The children in my classroom, 5A, coveted my school supplies and other things I had brought from Argentina: pens, pencils, markers, tempera colors, watercolors, comic books, and my beloved car collection. I gave all of it away with much more pleasure than I took from owning it. It was such a treat to see my classmates faces light up for an instant; the faces of those boys who were intrinsically just like me.

Chapter Ten

As far back as I can remember, I have taken great pleasure in giving. At that time giving acquired a different dimension because I was experimenting with the possibility of becoming someone who renounced his privileges instead of being comfortable with them and in that way making it clear that I was not much different from those who asked me for things. I was proud of being someone who liked to share, and in that way, at least, someone deserving being my dead uncle's nephew.

Every day our family had breakfast in the mezzanine because room service took almost an hour. I always ordered fried eggs and toast. The eggs that were served with a delicious baked ham, I placed in between three pieces of bread, wrapped them in a cloth napkin, and took them to school. I always gave one to the lady who fed the dogs and to the classmate who was the first to ask during recess. Eventually it became a game. When I walked out on the playground someone would yell *"¡Abierto!"* ("open!"). Whoever said *"¡Cerrado!"* ("closed!") before the others could say "¡Abierto!" got the prize, now coveted in my school, of the ham-and-egg delicacy.

It would have been acceptable for me to keep my treasures to myself without being thought a glutton, but I never did it those first few months. I loved to see my classmate's faces as they ate and enjoyed their sandwich! A sandwich made by my hands and stolen from the luxurious hotel kitchen to be delivered where it was most needed and certainly most desired.

The only one of my classmates that never asked me for a marker, a comic book, a car, or a piece of bread, but who enjoyed just being in my company was Evelio. At first he approached me the same way Scarpino had in Buenos Aires. He had offered to take care of my cat in his neighborhood. He and Fernando were my friends, my loyal friends, during those times in Havana. Fernando was my hotel friend, a friend in opulence but with the same generous spirit as myself. Evelio, skinny with green eyes, was born in Marianao in a rough neighborhood. At that time, he was living on Twenty First and J Street in El Vedado, in a huge house that had been abandoned by a rich man who had fled the country during the first years of the revolution, and was now shared by several families.

Evelio lived there with his mother, stepfather, and his older brother in a room that his stepfather had remodeled with a barbacoa, supplementing a mezzanine level over the ground floor to add more room to the space. Barbacoas in Cuba were made of wood, similar to those found in Helsinski but aesthetically different. Elsa, Evelio's mother, invited me to lunch one day and I took my kitten. She told me that they had eaten a cat once. She said it hadn't tasted too bad. Elsa had a genuine smile and contagious laughter and I felt very much at home in their home; I loved the fried eggs and rice that she fixed for me. The hotel could not come close to making eggs and rice with such exquisite flavor, nor did they have Elsa's well-cured frying pan. My mother had once called me Captain Kitten Batman when I was a little boy. When my parents grew so far apart from me that they couldn't even hear the sound of my voice, it was a kitten who took me inside the homes of my two best friends on the island: my hotel friend and my city friend. My father started his revolutionary training. We were told he was working in the Cuban petroleum industry. He had to be gone during the workweek. He would leave early Monday mornings and come home Fridays in the late afternoon. I had started to experience frequent nightmares of being chased, of hiding untold secrets, and found refuge only in the light of day.

My father no longer visited our suite at the hotel, not even on weekends. We didn't play together as we had in Portela. He didn't ask me to go with him to the mechanic's to pick up his Mendicream truck as he had in Argentina. He wouldn't look me in the eyes. He stopped seeing me, as if having been struck with Retinitis Pigmentosa—he could no longer access his peripheral vision. I would call to him: "¡Papá!" When we had embarked from Chile, he could still see me. Although at the beginning of his distancing, my image became blurred and unfocused in his eyes, he was still able to focus on me on occasion. I watched him as I disappeared, unable to discern that he was approaching a moment when he would no longer see me at all.

When I called to him, I had to struggle infinitely harder with my tone of voice or gestures in order to be seen, to ensure he detected my presence. Raising my voice no longer worked, and I began to call attention to myself in any way I could. If I wasn't enough for him as I was, then I had to change, and since I couldn't be a better child than I already was, I became a troublemaker. Being an amateur in this area, at first the trouble I got into was negligible.

Having become an invisible or at most an unrecognizable spot on the horizon of my parents' life, I began to behave as such.

I wanted my behavior to motivate third parties to make it clear to my parents that I was in need of their attention. I became a ghost who, having run out of options in his effort to be heard, resorted to frightening those around him.

In those days, I could have taken a pistol like the one in Che's house and carried it for longer, for days, in its holster. I think during the last few days my father spent in Cuba, I could have shot the gun; shot something that belonged to him without his noticing, at least not right away. I don't know if I could have shot him without his knowing, but for sure if I had shot myself, he wouldn't have noticed. Not right away, in any case. Not until someone brought it to his attention and then perhaps he would have said: "He died from a bullet wound? He died like a revolutionary!" So distracted would he be that he would ignore that a true revolutionary, a communist, would consider an act of suicide as shameful as an act of treason. We were living in a time when the Left presented a mask of solidarity. It was capable of conjuring the same cruelty as its opponent, the fascist Right. They thought themselves different, but anyone who could cross the street and observe them for a while would see two opponents wearing different color t-shirts, both the same size, both possessed by the same fury, the identical sullen expression on their faces, as they purposely walked hand-in-hand toward the end of the twentieth century.

One morning I asked my mother where my father was. She had told us that he had to work weekends now. At the end of the week, my mother asked me to come sit in her room and told me that she had to tell me something very important.

Bad news is always preceded by a certain energy one can feel. It's not necessary to be warned. My mother said: "Martín, I have to tell you something that perhaps you're not going to like to hear. Your father left for Argentina. He left to fight like your uncle Che, to fight for a better world and for a more progressive society where man can be free. I wanted to go with him, but it's my duty to stay here with my children."

At first I couldn't understand and I asked my mother how it was possible that he had left without saying goodbye. She told me that he hadn't wanted to wake us because he left at dawn. She said he had kissed us all on the forehead and that he had been very upset because he couldn't tell us good-bye. I asked her why he didn't wake us, it would have been so simple. She said:

"Martín, this didn't happen last night. It happened two weeks ago. He wasn't working for the oil company. He was preparing ideologically to go to meet his revolutionary destiny."

I couldn't understand that I had become so invisible as to not even deserve a more heartfelt good-bye than that. His goodbye didn't even give me the consolation of a memory. Was it possible that the roles had changed and he was the invisible one? After all, I had felt nothing when he kissed me that night. He must forgive me for being so lazy, that the imminence of our parting wasn't important enough to wake me from my sleep and get me out of bed! I felt a sense of loss that no child should ever have to feel. We were fatherless and our mother a sacrificial lamb who had been left to take care of herself and her children. Her dream of accompanying my father to his destiny and healing her marriage had collapsed. But I never made peace with her active conspiracy in all those lies that led to the loss of a father who parted without making sure I had felt his lips on my face.

It was then I knew why the fantasy of Santa Claus had ended several years before. It wasn't that my parents were as truthful as Copernicus with his thesis, or that they wanted to make me a part of an adult secret, as they had told me on that occasion. In truth, like everything in life, it was simpler than that. At the time, it had required less effort to concoct a lie than to tell me the truth.

Chapter Eleven

My first full- blown asthma attack occurred during my first month in Havana, and I was quickly driven to the hospital. The doctors thought it was caused by exposure to the carpet in my bedroom that accumulated dust, and perhaps some mold, from the humid climate of the island. In reality, asthma had been my companion since a year before I arrived in Havana. After I was released from the hospital, we moved to the twenty- first floor of the Habana Libre hotel where there were no carpets and even better views.

Shortly after my asthma attack, I made a second visit to the hospital. My aunt's husband had a Volkswagen Beetle. It was he who usually made the emergency trips required when one of the children in the family became ill or had an accident. This time I fell during a sleepwalking incident that had required my active participation. Before my head hit the floor, it encountered the corner of my brother's bed, where it stopped to pay its respects leaving part of my eyebrow behind. The damage was repaired with several stitches, and the family pointed out how lucky I had been not to lose an eye in that fall. I had been lucky. As lucky as an amputee who had dodged a fatal heart attack, or as lucky as anyone who had not been present when the bomb fell on Hiroshima.

No matter how serious my injury, I was always lucky that it had not been worse. But early on, I noticed that if my brother or sister got hurt, they were cuddled and pitied and the family lamented their terrible luck.

I suffered a second and more severe asthma attack when I became ill with bronchial pneumonia. This time I spent a week in the Pedro Borrás Astorga Children's Hospital.

The hospital was a beautifully appointed building amidst thick and colorful vegetation, and my doctor and the nurses all looked after me with great tenderness. My fever left me slowly and I enjoyed resting in such a safe and welcoming environment. The food I was served was unlike the food at the hotel. It was more typical of the food available to the average Cuban on the island, bland and simple. Still, I enjoyed its nearly absent flavor simply because of my very pleasant surroundings.

Almost all my memories are like that. Good people, good memories. I have a tendency to borrow the colors and the beauty of the places where I have been betrayed and use them to paint the places where I have been welcome and happy, experiencing no regret leaving those other places colorless.

Perhaps my memories of the Borrás Astorga are so dear to me because it was a beautiful building inhabited by people whose mission was to save others, and the simplicity of its food and its ambience free of artifices and lies, felt as good as dressing in pressed pajamas that smelled like the fresh outdoors.

From the hospital I was sent to a camp for children with asthma in Tarará, where years later the government constructed an international camp for Pioneros. The compound had three buildings: one for boys, one for girls, and a third for adult personnel. There were additional smaller buildings for different activities. The natural environment was spectacular and the beach was the best of all the ones I had seen. There was no comparison between the beach at Tarará and the beaches of the south Atlantic, or Barlovento, the beach we frequented the most. My brother came with me to the camp because he had suffered from asthma since he was a year old.

The camp was a healing place devoid of any indoctrination. We didn't attend school during the two weeks of our stay. We went swimming, we learned to row, took long walks on the beach, and were given natural remedies along with deep breathing exercises. Cuban medicine was well-versed in alternative therapies and used them much more than it was ever publically acknowledged, with excellent results. Although all the exercise we were exposed to did not cure our asthma, an asthmatic child who is having a good time has less time to complain about his health.

Being in contact with other children who also suffered from asthma and needed attention, if only medical, made me feel less of a foreigner in my new land. Sleeping away from home made the other children homesick, a feeling I had experienced before going to the clinic and gave us one more thing in common.

Our food at the camp was bland—neither good nor bad. It's possible that the staff tried to avoid our having any emotional reaction that a delicious meal might have evoked. My brother was ready to leave after our first day. I realized that not only could I not complain, but that I had a new role as the older brother, a role I was not at all fond of. At the camp, I became his defender from an insensitive teacher when she made fun of his

Argentinian accent. My brother gave me a grateful look. It had been a long time since we had really looked into each other's eyes. I thought that perhaps all of us were going blind.

Before the asthma attack that preceded my stay at the camp, I learned that my uncle Che suffered from asthma from the time he was a very young child and that his affliction influenced his desire to become a doctor as well as his determination to overcome every obstacle that was put in his path.

Most people think that asthma makes the intake of breath impossible. In reality, it makes it difficult to expel one's breath and causes a buildup of carbon dioxide in our system. In my case, asthma began to influence my character in a negative way. It began to fill me with rage. I kicked tree trunks, put my fist through walls, screamed impotently to whoever was near. But my asthma never offered me any gifts. Since it appeared at age nine, it has been an uncomfortable companion, a detested companion, albeit a very respected one.

Che, according to my family and his friends, only played harder when he fell victim to an asthma attack. It made me think of him as some unreal being, a comic-book character of sorts. There was no one at our camp who could box, run, or play baseball in the middle of an asthma attack. I understood that emulating his friends that did not suffer his ailment strengthened his resolve, but I found it difficult to imagine anyone in that state playing soccer or rugby. I wasn't sure I admired him for doing this. I was so different. When my bronchial tubes closed and made it difficult for me to expel my breath, my abilities and my strength were affected and I had no desire for accomplishment. I had no strength to chase a ball, or an ideal.

One day at the camp we were being taught boxing, when I was partnered with an African American boy whom I called "Ten." Ten was the number on his t-shirt and the number he answered to during roll call. In the boxing ring, Ten and I sparred. In the second round, I won the fight. I raised my hands happily, surprised that I had won. Ten was upset. He had only stopped fighting because my glove had hurt his eye and he wanted to go on. I took my gloves off quickly before anyone could change their mind about the outcome of the fight, and went to him to tell him that it was all right, that winning and losing weren't as important as giving our best to the game.

At that moment I reached out and touched Ten's hair. From the time I stepped on Cuban soil and saw the African Cuban bag-handler, I had wanted to touch their hair. I had seen Africans on TV in Argentina on programs like Tarzan and Daktari. Besides the color of their skin, the shape of their nose, the musculature of the men and the wide hips of the women, I had noticed their hair. At first glance it looked easy to care for, as if one could get up in the morning, give it the shape one wanted and not worry about it for the rest of the day. Raised to be polite, I resisted the temptation to touch the hair of the hotel employees, but after boxing with Ten, I asked if I could touch his hair. He looked surprised, but he agreed to allow my curiosity to be satisfied. Touching his hair was like touching a thick carpet. It seemed like excellent hair to be able to comb once a day without the need to use water or any other product to make it stay in place. My curiosity having been satisfied, I never gave it another thought.

In Tarará I enjoyed the sunshine, learned to play baseball, and began to feel like a Cuban during what turned out to be a fifteen-day stay.

My brother had a great time. I thought his fragile appearance, his being slight of build and shorter than I, might make it more difficult for him to adjust, but that inspired most of the teachers to be protective of him. In contrast, I'm not sure what it was about my demeanor that made others think I was so strong.

In those years, I could have benefited by being the recipient of at least some modicum of protection from the adults around me.

Ten and I continued our friendship for a short time after camp was over. He went to visit me at the hotel, but the red tape that included obtaining a permit a couple of hours before the visit, and waiting in the lobby until I came to escort him, made the process too complicated for our short pugilistic friendship to survive.

One day I went to Zorrilla, the hotel administrator, and asked him why he made it so difficult for Ten to visit me, since my mother had given me permission to see him. He smiled, and as if I were his nephew, he tousled my hair. I don't think Zorrilla wanted to know the texture of my dark straight hair. I began to see that our privileged way of life at the hotel, so different from the life of Cuban citizens, required great discretion so that it did not become known outside hotel walls.

The lack of courtesy extended to my friend, whether it was because of the color of his skin, because of his condition as an unknown member of the working class, or whether it was indeed because, as the hotel claimed, this was a practice in all five-star hotels around the world, did nothing to make me warm up to the ideals of this new society I lived in.

I never excelled in sports, although I didn't lack the ability to play them well. When I wanted to, I played volleyball and squash and I could be faster than most of my friends in swimming competitions. But I only played for enjoyment. I never understood why I should expend energy doing something that gave me no pleasure. For me, finishing something simply because I had started it, only applied to chess and ping-pong tournaments.

My teachers, family members, and those people whose job was my indoctrination that began to show up in my life more and more consistently, insisted that sports were an integral part of the formation of a revolutionary character regardless of one's health. I was not very interested in their opinion.

Photos, with notes by Martín Guevara

My great-grandparents, Roberto Guevara Castro and Ana Lynch Ortiz, with their children. Circa 1900.

With my mother and father, in Buenos Aires. 1963.
© Martín Guevara.

Riding El Doradillo in Portela, Buenos Aires. 1969.
© Martín Guevara.

4

Newspaper photo of my
father, Juan Martín, when
arrested, in handcuffs.
Argentina. 1974.

5

Fidel visits the Argentinian Industry exhibit in Havana. I am the child in
the background. This picture was taken on the day I asked him to help
my father get out of prison in Argentina. 1974. © Martín Guevara.

In the pool of the Hotel Habana Libre. 1975. © Martín Guevara.

With my grandmother, Elena, and my brother and sister. A framed photo of young Che on the wall watches over us. 1977. © Martín Guevara.

In Artemisa, in the mandatory work-study program, La Escuela al Aire, near Habana. 1979. © Martín Guevara.

With my friend, Nene, in the Castillo de Jagua, in the suburb of el Vedado in Havana. 1980. © Martín Guevara.

My grandfather, Ernesto.
1984. © Martín Guevara.

My father and my aunt, Celia,
having dinner at a friend's house.
1987. © Martín Guevara.

My friend, Evelio. 1988.
© Martín Guevara.

Dinner with my father in San Isidro,
Buenos Aires. 1993. © Martín Guevara.

Chapter Twelve

Back in school I continued my friendship with Evelio.

Sometimes I visited his house after school. We spent our time talking about the countries that we wanted to travel to, the goings on in his neighborhood, the fights that I saw him win on the playground, and sports, yet I never felt comfortable talking with him about a subject that had become very important to me: girls. Although Evelio had a girlfriend, I found that I was more comfortable discussing the subject of girls with my new friend Aming. Aming was my classmate. His mother was the daughter of Chinese immigrants who settled in Cuba after escaping the Maoist Revolution. They joined the Chinese community in Cuba, and started a business. Just when they began to enjoy the fruits of their labor providing them some economic freedom, the Cuban Revolution came to pass. It seemed bad karma or a curse pursued them. Only the Chinese temperament could survive both experiences, Mao and Fidel, without losing their minds. Aming and I talked almost exclusively about girls. He had a girlfriend, but I had not worked up the courage to ask any girl to be mine.

I had developed a feverish attraction to my friend Pedrito's sister. Pedrito lived at the hotel, the son of Argentinian exiles, and we had become good friends. I spent a lot of time with him at his apartment playing, always hoping for a glimpse of his sister, or for the rare occasions when she joined our games. Casual contact when we played together filled me with pleasure. Aming insisted that I tell her how I felt. But I would always come up with an excuse why I couldn't do so. Finally I told him that she already had a boyfriend. Aming still teased me and dared me to tell her, saying if I didn't I was being a mouse. But I didn't care what Aming thought. Perhaps for that reason I had chosen him to be my confidant. What he thought would have no consequence in my circle of friends, and he had never met Pedrito or his sister.

In time Aming became a very close friend, and I alternated after school visits between his house and Evelio's house. Aming's mother offered us treats from her kitchen. Besides being a good cook, she was also a beautiful exotic woman, and I liked looking at her. The subject of manhood was important in Cuba not only for adults but also for adolescents and children. The Revolution contributed to that image. A man who had no balls to fight against tyranny was a man who did not deserve to be considered a man. Once the revolution triumphed, the definition of manhood changed. Under the illusion that tyranny had disappeared, being a man became synonymous with following revolutionary doctrine and turning your friends and neighbors in to the authorities if they appeared to be involved in suspicious activities.

Manhood was also defined in terms of one's willingness to shed blood outside the country while propagating the ideals of the Revolution. Virility, that ephemeral mantel without which men were no longer safe, was synonymous with bravery in Cuba. Homosexuality was not tolerated on the island. After the new dining room was built in our school, we never again had to march single file to the Montori School's dining room. But shortly before the new dining room's inauguration there was an incident that taught me that in addition to people who were referred to as "worms," those who did not like the Revolution, there was a category in Cuba that no one defended. No one. Not even Evelio. Every day at noon recess, a heavyset boy went out to the playground. He had a very soft voice, very feminine movements, and liked to spend his time with the girls playing jump rope. One day, Medina the class bully and some of his friends, began to push him. The woman in charge of our supervision who was standing at the entrance to the patio told them not to bother him. Medina and his friends walked away for a moment but soon they returned to torment him. Medina kicked him, other boys slapped him, and I stood there frozen in place wondering why no one moved to defend the boy whose eyes were clearly imploring for mercy.

It was the girls who came to his rescue. They stood in front of him forming a protective wall Medina and his friends would not cross and managed to save him from the not-so-hard but very humiliating beating at the hands of his classmates. I asked my friend Aming if we should defend the boy and he said: "No! Are you crazy? They're going to think that you're a homosexual too!" When I saw Evelio that afternoon I told him what happened, and I asked if he thought Aming had advised me well. He said that he would sooner defend a Jehovah's Witness than that boy, because although the boy had undeniably been abused, the boy was a goose. I found it curious that in Cuban street language there were so many animal names used to refer to homosexuals. Fish names like pargo and grouper were commonly used, and more often they were referred to as "bird" or "goose." Lesbians were known by only one word: *"tortilleras."*

Being gay in Cuba was more dangerous than being a counter-revolutionary.

The Jehovah's Witness was in grade 4B. One day our redheaded teacher, Etelvina, hit Lázaro on the head. Lázaro was not a very good student and he was not very intelligent, but he was very well-behaved. When he didn't understand something, he preferred to be quiet instead of raising his hand to ask a question, because he had become aware that his teacher didn't like him. He suspected that Etelvina was not going to take the time to explain things to him until he understood them. She was more likely to shame him in front of everyone.

Sometimes Etelvina would ask Lázaro to write a sentence on the blackboard so that people would see how slow he was. She would ask him to write, "I have to listen to my teacher." ten times or more, while she hit him on top of his head with her knuckles. Once Etelvina caught him talking with his friend during class and she instructed him to go to the blackboard and write: "I must not talk in class." Before he was finished with the first sentence, everyone began to laugh. Etelvina turned towards Lázaro to see why his classmates were laughing, and saw that he had misspelled the word "talk." She told him in a loud voice: "You are so stupid!" while hitting his head again and again, harder and harder. She then ordered him to go sit down and told him that he was so dumb that it was impossible to teach him anything. Lázaro began to cry. He couldn't take the abuse any more and neither could I. I got up and confronted Etelvina and asked her how she could possibly do such a thing. I told her that she was a racist and that the only reason she hit Lázaro was because he had dark skin. There was a boy named Guido in the class who was a much slower learner than Lázaro. Etelvina treated him very well because he brought her little bottles of perfume his father bought on his trips to other countries. His slowness never seemed to bother her, and she laughed at all of his jokes. I thought Etelvina's veins would pop when I spoke out in

Lázaro's defense! She said: "Guevara, go to the office!" Just then Evelio got up and said: "Send me to the office also! I saw the same thing that Guevara did." That is how I ended up in the principal's office as the defender instead of the accused, as my teacher had wanted me to be. The principal asked me to write down what I witnessed but I refused, because I wasn't sure about the line that separated the truth from my suspicion, but I almost did. In the next few days, the skinny redheaded teacher glared at me with hatred in her eyes, but she did not hit or humiliate Lázaro ever again.

In Cuba, several years prior to our arrival, there had been a cleansing of all elements that could be considered a threat to the Revolution. These included activists who attempted to defeat the government, even poets who did not agree with the tenants of the revolution. Businessmen, philosophers, economists, lawyers, rebels who had fought for the revolution but had differences with the official government were dealt with, as were religions and the religious. Practicing Christians weren't jailed like others, but in a Marxist-Leninist society it was understood there was no place for believers of any other doctrine.

No laws were passed to forbid religion, but young people knew the moment they were identified as religious, their bosses, co-workers, and the police would turn against them. They would indeed have to be devout to rely only in Christ the Lord, for from that day on they would find it hard to get a raise no matter how hard they worked, and they would never be allowed to own a car, or an air conditioner, as these were perks reserved almost totally for party militants. Those who professed their beliefs in anything other than the Revolution would have the doors of paradise open to them, but it was known that all other doors were closed to them forever.

The Catholic religion had its churches and licenses to function. It even had some priests. But the faithful preferred to be cautious and did not parade their beliefs on the street. Older believers, those who had nothing left to lose, were usually the only ones to attend Mass. No religion was well tolerated then, but those who were tolerated the least were the Jehovah's Witnesses. Their religious practices made the authorities grit their teeth in anger.

The Jehovah's Witnesses did not salute any flag, did not sing hymns, and did not recognize borders. They saw themselves as children of God, and they would not pledge allegiance to any country on earth. There were no intermediaries between them and their God.

My friend Lázaro was like a martyr. Every morning, following the rules his parents taught him, parents who were seemingly not worried about their son's traumatic experiences, stayed silent during the singing of the National Anthem. Lázaro did not salute the flag, and of course, even though his religion never forbid it, he didn't join in the daily morning routine of declaring that he would be like my uncle Che. I never saw him laugh. Teachers harassed him and gave him bad grades, and they called his parents to come to the school on the pretense of some rule that he had broken. Although his religious freedom appeared to be tolerated, in reality Lázaro was being worn down morally and psychologically every day. He was constantly accused of treason against his country, was publicly disrespected, as was his family, and was ostracized by his classmates who did not want to join him in disgrace. There was no room on the island for a religious inclination that discounted the possibility of being exclusively devoted to Fidel as the only living deity, and of Che, Camilo, Marx, Lenin and Mella, who already resided in the Cuban version of Mount Olympus. When I first met Lázaro his posture was straight all day, as if in a stance of resistance or defiance. During recess only a few of us played with him. I felt a profound respect for his courage to confront the daily stress. But slowly I watched his frown grow deeper, and in a short time I could see the light go out of his eyes. One day, he stopped coming to school. In time we learned that Lázaro had suffered severe panic attacks that eventually became agoraphobia.

A few months after he left school, he and his parents left the island for the United States where all the gusanos went. Gusanos were the so-called worms that didn't embrace Fidel and his Revolution. Lázaro was rebuked in absentia at one of our daily morning meetings. I could not help but feel absolute solidarity with him when I became aware of our similarities. We both had been forced to abandon our country because of our parents' beliefs. The difference was that he could find no refuge in his school from his teachers who should have been his protectors. Instead they robbed him of his smile and turned their backs on him. Even if the day he left his country had been his birthday, he would not have found cake to take to the airport, or anyone who dared accompany him there to blow out his candles.

Chapter Thirteen

Inside the hotel life continued, divorced from the harsh reality being experienced outside its walls.

My maternal grandmother Elena arrived at the beginning of 1974. We were so happy to see her! All three of us wanted her to live with us forever. But she only stayed for a month and a half and spent her time mending clothes that could not be replaced, dressing us in the mornings before we left for school, and generally spoiling us. She wasn't the type of grandmother that drowned us in kisses and gave us compliments, but when she looked me in the eye, when she was sitting quietly after working in the house all day, her eyes told me: "I remember when you were little and you only wanted to come to our house on Cochabamba Street so that I could make you toast and butter and sweets and let you play your solitary games." She brought us gifts when she arrived in Cuba, gifts from my aunts, from my mother's cousins, and gifts from my father, whom she had seen in Argentina. She told us he was doing very well, but she also said she didn't see him often. Our gifts were very important, as many of them were fine clothes to replace our worn ones. We were living in a luxury hotel in Havana and had been taken to the best beaches, had eaten exquisite foods no longer available to the average Cuban, but finding clothes made by hand after 1961, clothes that looked even slightly fashionable, was impossible. Buying clothing in Cuba at that time ensured that you would be wearing the same clothes as a third of the Cuban population.

In Cuba at that time, things were found in groups of threes. Some things like screwdrivers, hammers, tweezers, or house paint could not be found at all. Hardware-store aisles were practically empty, and salespeople spent their days talking to their friends on the phone or gossiping. People resorted to stealing tools at work. In this way, one could find almost anything except clothing, soaps, or rationed food. Those had to be obtained in stores on a given day of the week with a special number, and one could choose from three different styles, three different colors or sizes, all having in common the absence of aesthetics. Chiclets, comic books, colored pencils, ink pens, musical instruments, dolls, toy guns, bows and arrows, and mountain bikes were not available at all. They had to come from outside the country. And that was the distinctive trait of the bourgeoisie in a communist country: having the things that came from a capitalistic country was a privilege reserved for the ruling class. Ironic. My grandmother's visit allowed us not to dress in the drab costume of the average Cuban, thus keeping our identity as foreigners intact. The kids in the Habana Libre liked to appear as if they had only recently arrived in the country. They acted as if they still had Chiclets. In the hotel, you could not allow yourself to be defeated by the city. Living in the Habana Libre had nothing to do with exile, really. It was a status symbol. The time came when I stopped caring about fashion, when I began to yearn for meaning in my life, for a relief of day after sad day that followed each other without relief. And the need for relief stemmed from two

Shadow of a Myth 83

pieces of news that my mother had delivered. One was that we would not go back to Argentina for some time, maybe for a couple of years. Before I could explode with anger at those words, she added: "Your father has been taken prisoner." My father was in prison. My father spent his nights in prison. I could barely breathe. My father was in prison. He left me without saying good-bye. He had not mentioned that he was leaving, had not answered my letters begging him to return or asking him to let me join him. I was so hurt that he did not write! And then my mother told me that he had been in prison for weeks. Fury and helplessness overtook me. My mother couldn't stop me. She didn't know how, nor did she have much interest in learning how. The walls of the hotel could not contain me. None of my friends showed up to take me to a hospital for mortally wounded children whose souls felt cold, a place where perhaps someone could warm me. The son of my grandfather Ernesto, Che's brother, my mother's husband, my father and the father of my siblings was in prison.

Who was this man, my father? I could not stay angry at his indifference. As a child I thought parents had children in order to take care of them and to make the children happy. That day I stopped believing my own story and instead clearly saw that the world does not belong to the children. I found out that while I waited for his letters or for him to send me Chiclets and t-shirts, my father was involved in the much more important mission of helping to create a socialist movement in our native country of Argentina. He spent his time recruiting people, making pamphlets, gathering with like-minded people. Fighting? I didn't know. I was glad the worst hadn't happened. He wasn't dead. I should have been happy that he was alive. On the same day I also learned that my grandmother Elena would soon return from Argentina with even more supplies and in the company of my beloved aunt Celia, my uncle Che's sister. My father was in prison for being a militant in a socialist party and for his relationship to his brother Che. Repression in Argentina was worsening. When Aunt Celia finally arrived, she assured us that my father would be freed soon. She told us that he had been imprisoned because they found him carrying Marxist pamphlets, but that excellent lawyers were defending him. My aunt was the same as always, just like my grandmother. I was not surprised that they had traveled together.

My aunt Celia was perhaps the bravest, most energetic person I knew. She didn't conform to a mold, and she was someone I could always count on. I needed her then. I started writing letters to my father, addressing my letters to his jail.

Chapter Fourteen

One afternoon I was returning to the hotel from J and Twenty-First streets, after leaving my friend Evelio's house. As I was passing Coopelia, the famous ice cream store in Havana, I heard two shots. People ran in all directions. Some threw themselves on the ground. I remained standing, frozen in surprise, not bravery. A man dressed in white from head to toe held a pistol in his hand. His victim lay on the concrete on Twenty Third Avenue, not moving. The police came. I stayed and watched from a distance as people got up from where they had dropped to the ground and went on their way.

A heavy-set woman dressed in white and wearing a white handkerchief on her head that was as white as her teeth, was explaining to a small group near me that the shooting had been an act of reparation, that the man who had been shot had humiliated someone. I didn't understand what she meant. The woman was an "Abacuá" and I asked her what that meant. She said it meant she belonged to a sect of the descendants of slaves.

In Havana there was a rumor that every New Year's Day, Fidel and his ministers would gather to listen to the Abacuá's predictions. I had once overheard some people say that Fidel was always interested in their predictions regarding his health. Those predictions appear to have been true.

I left the scene in a hurry, anxious to get to the hotel and tell my family what I had witnessed. But when I arrived, an unexpected sight distracted me. A new guest had arrived. She was surrounded by people who were speaking almost exclusively with her. She was seated at a table for six. She was a tall woman, with long blond hair and a beautiful face. I don't know if it was her charm or if it was the manner in which others spoke to her, but I felt that I was under her spell.

I noticed that she spoke English. I overheard a hotel guest telling her friend that the American was a famous actress. I had never seen her in a movie, but now I was anxious to see one of her movies as soon as possible.

Soon my family came down for dinner and I joined them. I was mesmerized by the blonde actress across from us and never got around to sharing the story of my adventure near Coopelia. Before dessert came I got up to use the bathroom and walked slowly past the blonde's table. She looked my way and waved at me, and I approached her. I said hello. I found I could say nothing else. I stayed near her table more time than I should have, thinking how beautiful she was, but I never allowed my mouth to form the words, and she gave me a friendly smile and went back to her conversation with her friends. Back at our table I felt good because I had managed to speak with her, but sad that I couldn't tell her what I wanted to say. The guest was Candice Bergen. She remained on the island a few days to show her support of progressive causes. I would have liked to ask her if she saw what she expected to see on the island. The hotel had many famous visitors, but I knew few of them. I didn't know of

Shadow of a Myth

their influence until many years had passed. In the majority of cases, their fame was due to some form of political idealism in support of the Cuban Revolution. The government of Argentina in coordination with the government of Cuba organized an event in Havana to show off the success of the Revolution. My mother received an invitation, as did the mothers of my friends Fernando and Pedrito, and the three of us spent three days going to the fair. The fair wasn't especially fun for kids or adolescents, but what made it fun for me was that I got to go there with my friends. On the last day of the fair two chauffeurs dressed in olive green came to pick us up in a Volga. When we arrived at the venue, we saw a Chaika among the other cars and immediately recognized the typical chaos that took over when Fidel arrived anywhere. He arrived accompanied by Osvaldo Dorticós, officially the president of Cuba at that time. They were greeted by two Argentinians who were there representing their government and together they began a tour of the facility. Fidel listened intently to what he was being told. I looked at them both the whole time, surprised by the interest that Fidel seemed to have in everything around him. I liked that Dorticós was wearing a suit. I hadn't seen one since I left Argentina. In Cuba, dignitaries dressed in olive green, or in formal guayaberas made of linen with long sleeves. But Dorticós allowed himself the occasional suit when he thought it appropriate. I was standing right by Fidel. I wanted to touch his gun but the bodyguard next to him was watching me intently. An Argentinian reporter held Fidel's attention, firing questions at him that seemed to never end. The reporter kept trying to get me out of the way so he could step closer to Fidel until I finally said to him out loud: "Would you please stop bothering me?" Silence followed my question, and people looked at the reporter defiantly. Nonplussed, the man continued his work from a distance. Once in the hallway, Fidel put his hand on my shoulder, and on my head as we walked side by side. When we were leaving the meat exhibition and headed for where the grains were being shown I pulled on his jacket until he had no graceful way of avoiding bending over towards me. He asked me what I wanted. I looked around and saw newsmen, bodyguards, businessmen, all looking at us attentively. I headed for a corner of the room taking him with me and once there he had the courtesy to get down on his knee so his head and my face were close together. I got really close to him because I didn't want anyone to overhear my words. We were together for a while, and as I stood and he knelt next to me, we quietly spoke. I told him I was Martín Guevara, son of Juan Martín. In my innocence, I didn't realize that he knew who I was. A fly didn't approach Fidel without his knowing its DNA and family history. Later I was glad he had given me more time than he had given the reporter and most importantly that he had made me a promise. I was content with that promise and we began to walk back to the crowd and slowly became separated by some distance. It felt good to have had some time with the leader of Cuba in public. That night I didn't sleep but I was feeling particularly hopeful. Although my anger at my father for leaving me without saying goodbye might have contributed to his bad luck, I had spoken with Fidel, a man who had the power of a king and the influence of the gods, and we had exchanged words that promised to give me and my family some peace.

CHAPTER FIFTEEN

One afternoon I left school in a hurry and almost ran to the hotel. I was eager to go to the room, change clothes, and head for the swimming pool where my growing group of friends waited.

Because I was distracted, I didn't notice the tall man walking towards me in the lobby and ran right into him. I immediately apologized. He asked me my name, and when I told him he said his name was Dean Reed. He told me he was a Rock-and-Roll singer, and I noticed that he spoke with an American accent. I had listened to the Beatles and other Rock groups when I lived in Argentina. The man realized that I was awed at meeting a real American Rock-and-Roll singer, and he invited me to sit with him. He told me that he was an American who loved his country very much. But he said he didn't like the government of the United States. He made it clear that he was a communist and asked: "I imagine you're a communist too?" I told him I was. "I am a communist just like my uncle Che." He asked me to wait for him while he got something from his room, and he returned with a 45-rpm record. He signed it and gave it to me. I thanked him and told him about my other American friends who lived on the island. Later I wondered if that had been a good idea. None of the prominent guests visiting or living in Cuba at that time had given me permission to divulge their presence there to the first American Rock-and-Roll singer I met in the lobby of my hotel.

Soon, our hotel welcomed another notable guest, a man who would add more color to our already-colorful community. After his life was repeatedly threatened by bombings and a few close calls with bullets, my grandfather Ernesto decided it was time to leave his country and take refuge in Cuba. Cuba was the island that had made his oldest son famous and where he knew he would be treated with deference because his presence on the island would contradict the growing suspicion that Fidel was responsible for orchestrating the circumstances that led to Che's death. When he arrived, he told us that my father had been freed. My happiness was almost complete except for a small detail. My father would not be returning to Cuba. He had to stay in Argentina where he was needed.

My grandfather was happy to be with us. His much younger wife and his two small children, my new aunt and uncle, accompanied him.

The week before the worst hurricane of the year, my mother told me that after a few months of freedom, my father had been captured again and that this time it would be much more difficult for him to obtain his release. Then she said: "Martín, Cuba is our home now. We will not be going back to Argentina." I asked my mother a million questions trying to find out why we would not be going back home, but all she could say to me was that it was dangerous for us there now. I didn't want to accept that stepping on my native soil, attending my school, would be dangerous. Dangerous because of what my parents did. Dangerous

Shadow of a Myth

because I was the nephew of an uncle I had never met. I was angry, and my heart felt as if it had been nourished by dynamite. None of that had anything to do with me. Revolutions and prisons were as foreign to me as the Russian language, cricket games, or elephant races. I was sick of it all. How could I respect and approve of what my uncle or my father had done if that meant I was not safe in my own country with my friends? How could I be so ignorant as to blind myself to the damage that had been done to my life? They wanted me to be happy and proud of my fortune. Yes, of course, and also they wanted me to grow into an honorable man so that the day I was needed in the international scenario I could answer the call of destiny. Well, in reality, that was what revolutionaries were supposed to feel. But the fact was that none of the children who had been close to the major figures of the Revolution would get any closer to a front line than attending a party at an embassy, or scoring a front-row seat at one of Fidel's interminable speeches. My grandfather followed me to my room, and sat across from me trying to calm me down. He spoke to me gently and caressed my head slowly, waiting for me to regain my composure. When my sobbing receded and I could finally breathe, he explained that my father met a woman in the Argentinian underground, and that the night he left the hotel without my knowing it, he knew that he was leaving us behind for good. Not because of the woman that now fought by his side, but because he had a commitment to honor: a commitment to fight for social change in Argentina as his brother had fought before him in Cuba. He said that the commitment my father made to follow in his brother's footsteps put us in grave danger in our country. He said my father was protecting us from unnecessary risks in telling us not to join him in Argentina. My grandfather swore to me that day that he would always be there for me when I needed him, as if he were my father. And although that was not a binding promise, the simple fact that he said those words brought me a sense of warmth that had a calming effect on my troubled heart. That night I wasn't worried about what my mother felt, but I had no choice but to think of her as a victim, given her state of depression. Her job in the magazine *Mujeres*, keeping company with her French friend Annie—nothing seemed to pull her out of her darkness. She was angry at my father who had abandoned her for what she thought was a revolution in Argentina, when the truth was that he couldn't stand to spend another day with her or with her children. My father was taking a grave risk in his decision to help the poor of the world. But that didn't excuse his behavior towards us. I thought that it would be convenient for us all to have our own poor person handy, so that we could use him as an excuse to abandon everything when things got difficult in our own homes. That day, finding out after two years in Cuba that my parents' marriage was over forever, that he would not come back because he was making a new family with another woman, I had little time to process the information. Hotel workers kept knocking at our door asking permission to come in and place tape on the glass windows that faced the balcony. It was a feeble attempt to contain the hurricane that was predicted to arrive with unusual fury. From my room on one of the highest floors of the hotel, I hoped to watch the hurricane destroy everything in its path.

Chapter Sixteen

My paternal aunt Ana María, Che's sister, her husband Fernando, and my cousins Juan and Rosario, were the first to leave the hotel. They had been the first familiar faces I saw when I arrived in Havana, and we had shared many wonderful as well as trying times together. After three months in a beautiful house near the famous Tropicana Night Club in Havana, we received news that they had decided to move to Rome, Italy.

Were they growing tired of socialism? I understood that it would not have been appropriate or particularly safe for them to express those feelings out loud. They could always give the impression that they would continue living the message of the Revolution in another country. They left us their Volkswagen. At the time, my mother was wallowing in her depressive state and hardly ever left the house except for an occasional stroll to the balcony to enjoy the ocean breezes, but it was good to have our own transportation in case of an emergency. In our living room we had some books that were written about my uncle Che. Some books told stories about his life, or in reality, about the myth that his life had become. Other books contained writings about Che's life from the point of view of Marxism. Everyone knew of my love of reading, and I wonder if the books were placed there for my edification. Curious to get to know this man who seemed to be so many different things, I read the books during my vacation.

Che was present in all things, but not so much the man himself, my uncle, as the process of his metamorphosis into sainthood. He was becoming a communist saint, an unfeeling statue impervious to pain, a tough as nails human being who was untouched by fear, or by temptation, or by pleasure. He had become a martyr. As he grew in stature, I was conscious of my duty to emulate him. Yet I felt there was still time before I had to decide whether to become a sainted martyr like my uncle or risk becoming something else entirely. Still, I was aware that I was not using that time well. I did, however, take the time to learn all I could about this man whose footsteps I was expected to follow. I knew stories about who my uncle had been before his public metamorphosis. Stories heard within the family, and outside the family from his close friends. My mind was captured by the ease of how someone could be so transformed after his death. Che was raised by a father whose businesses inevitably failed and by a mother who was obsessed with his education, and he grew up liking rugby, French poetry, and Argentinian politics. His parents encouraged in him a great sense of adventure as well as a tremendous fear of failure. He spent his adolescence and his youth without distinguishing himself in any way from his peers. Alberto Ferrer, Che's best friend from childhood, adolescence, and youth, wrote that Che, whom he always referred to by his first name Ernesto, "never lacked for attention from women." He was handsome, played soccer, he could swim very well, ride horses, was well read, and had memorized verses to recite to the girls he courted. He was a Guevara de La Serna, and his family name was an asset to him within his circle of friends. Ferrer says in his memoir that he and Che both lost their virginity with a Ferrer family maid, and later continued their sexual experimentation with her when she went to work for the Guevaras. It appears neither family ever knew.

Chichina Ferreyra, a serious girlfriend, said of Che in an interview: "Poor Ernesto. He never succeeded at anything! He was not a good doctor, or a good photographer, as he had wanted to be. He was definitely not successful as a government minister or as a fosterer of revolutions" yet she always remembers the first time she saw him walking down the street. He stood out so much that the fifteen-year-old Catholic school student recalls that upon seeing him she was at once filled with awe and fear.

I grew up hearing that my uncle liked French poetry, and philosophy. He became enamored of Marxist theory in his readings, but he was never politically affiliated with any party. He was also drawn to the emerging consciousness movement in India. He wrote about those subjects and others, including rugby, in his university's student newspaper. Unlike Chichina, I thought that not everything had turned out badly for my uncle. I thought it was quite an achievement to have kept an almost daily written record of his life in journals. His life seems to have been lived so that it made good copy. His writing suggests the soul of an author, of a born poet. What premonition made him leave behind so much of the story of his life? It was as if he knew that the world would one day want to know. Every photograph taken of him from any angle appeared to reflect his perfection. I studied his image carefully, looking in his eyes for answers about his truth. I sensed hatred of the enemy in some, and yet in his smile I intuited an infectious love of life.

Reading his diaries I was left with the impression that when he chose to follow the path of a warrior, he left behind the probability of becoming a very gifted writer.

My uncle was not fond of games except for chess, and he only admired European thinkers, mostly the French. He liked sports, books, thoughtful humor, and he was curious about the exploration of the human psyche. He was particularly fond of his own image, of his mother, and of traveling unfamiliar roads for the first time. He was sympathetic to destitute human beings who had no access to work, to food, to a life of dignity, and he loved horses.

He didn't like dances that weren't tangos, although that could be because he inherited the Guevara's inability to master the subtlety of dance. He didn't care for work much, and he didn't like people who complained or were not interested in politics, dandies, informants, or members of the bourgeoisie.

As I learned more about my uncle, it seemed that he was a contradiction. He was at the same time both a man whose life made it easy to construct a myth around him and also a man whose footsteps I could imagine running towards a precipice, a man devoid of a need for stability. And in this vision, I sensed in him a need to keep moving, perhaps a need to outrun his constant companion, the asthma that also pursued me. Maybe asthmatics prefer to breathe into an escape rather than accept another life sentence that we might deserve—like being able to face the clarity of truth.

I did not feel my uncle as a protective figure in my life. He lived stridently, and it is my opinion he was always too tied up inside with issues of his childhood, with Oedipal preoccupations. As I tried to find some communality between us, the bigness of his life made it impossible for me to rise to the challenge of imitation. I could not imagine myself climbing such a steep mountain.

I was beginning to see that the image Che projected had an enormous influence in the world, and on middle-class young

Shadow of a Myth

people who flirted with the Left during the 1960s and '70s. His image cast a giant shadow on my father's life, and as a consequence, on mine. His influence on my father had robbed me of an important presence in my life.

My father had been willing to sacrifice his life to emulate his brother. He took his duty seriously, and I am not sure that he took the time to contemplate the rightness or wrongness of his path. He paid for his loyalty dearly without once uttering a word of complaint, while other Guevaras slept in exile, seemingly free of the presence of phantoms in their nightmares. But I, his son, was finding myself more and more resistant to the task of living in bondage to the ideals of my uncle, the idol. I wasn't sure I would ever summon sympathy for a Revolution that had revolutionized my life, robbing me of so many people, places, and things that I loved. While contemplating the shrinking possibility of my greatness, I finished my primary school and spent the summer playing and getting into trouble with my friends from the hotel, Fernando, Ronnie, and Jessica. Ronnie and Jessica were the children of Huey Newton of the Black Panthers movement in the United States, who were also exiles like me. I suspected their father would not be happy to learn that I shared his presence there with the Rock singer Dean Reed.

My mother liked to tell stories about my escapades to her friends. I was the questionable hero of her stories as most of them were stories of how my friends and I managed to play tricks on the hotel guests. Her penchant for acting was obvious and grew as her audience grew. But I noticed that she talked about me as an interesting and daring character, while she spoke lovingly and gently of my brother and sister. Sometimes after one of her stories she would tell her audience what a psychologist once told her about me after a few sessions. She would say "and the doctor told me that Martín was either a genius or a moron, that time would tell. And so far, I see no signs of genius." She waited for her audience's laughter looking at me teasingly as if inviting me to join in. I would shrink my toes inside my shoes and allow my lips to almost form a smile, while looking for a quick escape through any adjoining door. Shortly before the summer ended my mother told me that I would be going to a secondary school called Amistad Cuba Canadá located in rural Quivicán, a half hour drive from Havana. My Revolutionary training would continue away from home, with my becoming a pupil in the Cuban Beca. My indoctrination would begin in earnest there, as I attended classes and learned a trade of my choice. The Cuban sun had darkened my skin, become one with it. My stomach craved black beans and garlic. It had been some time since I had felt desperate to return to Argentina, a while since the Cuban accent had been a challenge. But nothing had prepared me for the news that I would be sent to a Beca like other Cuban children.

I prayed I had heard wrong. "Not the Beca!" I begged the nonexistent gods for mercy. It had been another crazy whim of Cuban Socialism. The Beca students attended classes in the morning, but after lunch they were given a machete or a hoe to plow furrows in the fields and given a limited amount of time in which to do so. Most of them had only seen hoes and machetes in pictures. Now they were fixtures in their nightmares. The idea of being sent to live in the Beca began to dissolve the last ties that held me to my family, the last hopes of ever being the owner of my own life. Too soon after the news, the day came when my vacation ended and I had to dress in the blue uniform of the Beca and embark on the dreaded journey. The first day of school, we were all given three uniforms and a blue tie that substituted the handkerchiefs of the pioneers we had once been. We received a pair of black Russian boots, two pair of black Kiko brand plastic shoes, a heavy blue coat to protect us from the cold of the Quivicán winter, a few bars of soap, a towel, and shampoo. Any other supplies were to be brought from home. We were allowed to wear street clothes in the evenings after dinner. Half of the students worked the fields in the morning while the other half attended classes. In the afternoon the order would be reversed. Those of us in seventh grade, the first year of secondary school, started the day in class. After four hours, we went directly to the lunch-room, where we were given rice and beans, hard-boiled eggs and bread. At three thirty we gathered in the schoolyard, stood in straight lines, and climbed in the trucks that would take us to work in the field. My first job was planting strawberries. I weeded the field with my hoe, a task that seemed interminable in that field so overgrown with all things green, and planted so many strawberries there was no way to keep count.

Students who could not excel at schoolwork had an opportunity to excel in the fields by becoming brigade chiefs. Generally, the brigade chiefs were tall, sometimes kids that had been held back in school. They were stronger than most of us and they were able to attract the girls because of their physical strength.

We would see these boys, taller and stronger than most of us, when we showered after finishing our work. Most were fully developed and flaunted their maturity proudly. My friends, at age twelve or thirteen, still looked like boys, and still sounded like boys. Some of us had a few facial hairs but had not yet started to shave. We yearned for the day when we would begin to look like the others.

The first week a teacher told some of us that we would be sleeping in a room adjoining the hallway for a time until our dormitory was ready. About fifteen of us would sleep near the stairway that accessed the second floor. Nights were chaotic. Students would have boot fights, throwing their boots at each other after lights out, laughing when a boot surprised a sleeping student. Sometimes a group of kids would get together and slap or hit a sleeping classmate, quickly dispersing by the time he became fully awake. At times a stick or a belt was used to cause more injury. But I was most impressed when I watched cigarettes being lit between the toes of a sleeping student. When they felt the burn they instinctively reached for the cigarette butt and thus burned their hands also in the effort to stop the pain in their feet. All these things went on without interference from our teachers. One night I became the target of a group of boys who hit me. I woke up cursing loudly and they proceeded to beat me mercilessly. I pretended to fight back, purposely missing them and hitting nothing but air, afraid that connecting with anyone would increase the force of their blows. They only stopped when two teachers happened to enter and asked what had gone on. Two days later I was taken out of that temporary dorm. I wasn't sent home or to the home of a dignitary living nearby, but I was given a cot against a wall, for which I was extremely thankful. Onyx, the man who was in charge of our family, the one who had brought my Pionero uniform to me at the hotel before my first day of school in Cuba, told me that my father had asked the authorities to see to it that we were not treated any differently than other students.

He did not want us to be treated with deference, to have any privileges besides those to which we were entitled by the divine providence of being children of the Revolution. And although I myself had thought many times that we should not enjoy the privilege of living at the Hilton, I had certainly never wished to find myself in a secondary school in the country eating the same food and sleeping in a dormitory filled with a sense of the hopelessness of children robbed of their chance to delay their adulthood for a few more years. Why a secondary boarding school? My father wanted me, his firstborn, to emulate my uncle Che. He had instead provoked in me a hatred of communism.

Chapter Seventeen

In the same way that the Hotel remained impervious of the consequences of that drug called Revolution, the children of those in charge lived in a very peculiar system of equality. Their lives unfolded in marked contrast to a Marxist-Leninist upbringing. Every time I returned home on a weekend, I begged my mother to speak with the authorities so that I would be allowed to leave the Beca. I even asked my grandfather Ernesto to intercede. Both replied that it was my duty to my new country to stay, that the Beca was important for my Revolutionary formation. My frequent pleas fell on deaf ears.

My grandmother, trying to console me, would tell me stories of her town in Spain and of the hard winters she experienced there, of the games the children played. She described the harsh winters and the effects of the freezing temperatures, perhaps in an attempt to make my reality seem less severe. Instead I found myself envying the children in her small town, who went home after school to the warmth and love of a family that waited for them around the hearth of a two story red roofed house where they shared warm bread and listened to music, and where they slept in their own beds. I wasn't sure what combining work and study in a Beca would do for our bourgeoning Revolutionary spirits, but I knew for sure that productivity was not the primary objective of the training.

It was common to hear the guajiros complain. Once the backbone of the Cuban economy, farmers who worked the fields themselves, now some were in charge of transporting students. They bitterly complained that the students had no idea what needed to be done, that they were lazy, and made it a point to tell us and whoever would listen that we were destroying everything in our paths like a plague of insects.

Economically the Beca was a failure. Was it a success from the point of view of building character in young children? That seemed to be its true objective, to create a strong work ethic that would make us successful in the future. At the time and looking back I am not sure that the socialist/communist experiment succeeded. In addition to the asceticism to which I had been condemned by my father's wish that I imitate my uncle, and despite my being far away from my uncle's books in our living room and far away from the family we shared, it wasn't long before his presence caught up with me. When I arrived in the Beca, I made it a point to keep to myself. Caught between the violence that greeted me in my first dorm and the presence of so many pretty girls I wasn't comfortable approaching, I was feeling lonely except for one Argentinian friend who was also at the Beca. The girls would only speak to the good-looking and popular students, the ones that had already successfully navigated puberty. One day I went out to the yard and a group of girls walked up to me. One of the girls said: "Hey, you, Argentinian, what is your name?" "Martín" I said to her and her friends. "Martín, Haydée says that you are Che Guevara's nephew and we wanted to know... is that true?" I was hesitant to answer in

Shadow of a Myth

the affirmative. I could see in those girls' eyes an admiration I had not earned. I had been invisible to them before, and I was still invisible to them. It was Che they recognized. Yet, I felt a sudden gratitude to my uncle who had made it possible for the students who passed by us at that moment to see me speaking to the prettiest and most popular girls in my class. I temporarily lost my aversion to being known as the nephew of the myth. "Yes, my father is Ernesto's brother. Why?" The girls began asking questions that showed they were curious about my uncle, but also about me. The eighth-grade boys walked past and stopped to talk to us. The girls introduced me as Martín, the Argentinian, and I felt welcome by them. The prettiest girl in the group, a short slight blonde, watched me silently during this exchange. Her name was Mayté. She was getting a lot of attention from the eighth-grade boys. The boys left and I stayed with the girls, who decided it was time to smoke. Smoking was forbidden in our school, but at times we were quite loosely supervised during our recess. My instinctive reaction was to pass, since I had never held a cigarette between my fingers, but instead I asked for the cigarette and took a quick drag filling my mouth with a bitter-tasting smoke. I tried to hold the smoke inside my mouth so that I would not look inexperienced, but when I passed the cigarette to a classmate she looked at my face and broke into laughter. Mayté scolded her for making fun of me, and asked the girls if they had been born smoking. Then she asked me if it was the first time I smoked. I felt an almost imperious need to lie, but I had already proven I had no first-hand knowledge of cigarettes. Girl talk ensued, and I was no more adept at that than smoking. I excused myself and went to meet my friend Juanjo, and told him what had transpired. The groups of students around us started to disperse, as they headed for their dorms. As we got ready to go to bed, I saw a girl looking in my direction. She was holding a boy's hand. She caught my eye and winked at me, and then turned back to the guy that appeared to be her boyfriend. Juanjo caught the gesture. "I can't believe Mayté winked at you!" Without shame I lied to him: "I smoke with the girls in the afternoons." That night I felt better than I had since I arrived. The next day, we would go to Lenin Park on a field trip to Havana. Lenin Park, also known as the City Garden, was an ecological treasure. In addition to many species of birds and very well cared-for plants, there were restaurants, public swimming pools, and an aquarium. But the most important thing to everyone who frequented the park, was the availability of chocolate bars we called "peters." No chocolate was sold anywhere else in the city of Havana. At Lenin Park, one could buy chocolate without a ration card and buy as much as one wanted until the chocolate quickly ran out. People stood in line early in order to be sure that they were able to enjoy the exquisite experience of chocolate. All of us enjoyed the day, and I did so particularly, walking among a group of very good-looking girls. The next day Mayté and Haydée introduced me to the music they liked and tried, unsuccessfully, to teach me to dance. They listened to songs by singers that we were forbidden to listen to, like José Feliciano and Julio Iglesias. I didn't like either of them, but I was enjoying the attention. I liked groups like Grand Funk Railroad and The Rolling Stones. Those artists were also forbidden, their music considered subversive. In Cuba, things were either forbidden or they were required. A good Revolutionary listened only to Cuban music.

I was drawn to the forbidden music, not only because it was forbidden, but also because I liked the sound of the music, the look of the long-haired foreigners, and the juicy riffs of the rock guitars. The weekends brought the hope of a trip home. Every Friday night, I leaned on the balcony that overlooked the road to our school, waiting to catch a glimpse of my grandfather's car coming to pick me up. I hoped he would arrive before I had to spend another night in the dorm and miss half of Saturday morning at home. My grandfather had given me his word that he would pick me up. But many Fridays passed without my grandfather keeping his promise, and my friend Juanjo waited with me trying to give me hope with a not so convincing look. His look was one not of hope, but of compassion. One day we were told that Prime Minister Trudeau of Canada would be visiting the Beca with Fidel. For days we got ready. Every corner of the buildings was cleaned until the place was glistening. This happened each time Fidel was expected. But this time Fidel and Trudeau decided to do something more important than visiting a Beca in the middle of nowhere. A few days before, Barbara Walters, an American journalist, had been at the Beca, as part of the itinerary for her interview with Fidel. She asked Fidel to tell her about his loves, his girlfriends, his women, and Fidel said he never spoke of those things with the press. The powerful Caribbean pirate and the Blonde from the North couldn't keep their eyes off each other.

The day that Trudeau and Fidel didn't visit the Beca we were given new leather shoes and new ties. I strolled around all day with my new leather shoes and afterward I stood on a balcony and lit a cigarette. I had barely inhaled when I saw our principal approaching me and threw the cigarette from the balcony hoping it would not find a student on its way down. "Guevara, have you made some comments about our school to your family?" "No", I said. "Fidel didn't come to visit my grandfather this week." I was amused watching his expression move between surprise and incredulity. He had just had a very stressful day trying to make the school seem worthy of its anticipated visitors, and now was thrown off by my unexpected comment. My days at that Beca ended soon after. Someone stole a pair of pants and socks from me. That time I said nothing. I waited until everyone went to his or her classrooms and I stayed out of sight in the dining room. I went back to the dorm and stole as many pairs of socks as I could hold, kept the ones I liked and threw the rest in the toilet. I didn't flush the toilet because I wanted the socks to be found. I took several pairs of pants, soiled them with anything I could find, and threw them out the window towards the back of the dorm. I found a can of condensed milk in someone's suitcase, poked holes in it and drank what I wanted. The rest, I poured on the bed of the leader of the gang of thieves, soaking the bed cover and sheets. I left the dorm transformed. Even now I remember the emancipated feeling after the violence, a sort of liberation after months of fear.

Later, a classmate told my teacher that I had been late for one of my classes. I said that I had smoked a cigarette or two before going to class. But one of my teachers had spotted me leaving the dorm and I ended the day in the principal's office, where eventually I gave up on denial. I said I had retaliated that morning for all the times I had been offended in the past. I said I had never known anyone to get in trouble for stealing my things. I was driven to Havana in a school car with a note stating that I was to return accompanied by a member of my family. When I arrived at the hotel I told my mother what happened, and before she could scold me I reminded her of all the abuses I had put up with at the Beca: things stolen from me, being slapped in my sleep, the verbal abuse I endured, and I reminded her I had asked for her help many times and I got no help at all.

My mother called my grandfather Ernesto, and he and I drove to the Beca together. I spotted Juanjo on the balcony where we waited to be picked up on Friday nights, feeling ambivalent about the possibility that I might no longer get to spend time with him if I was expelled. The principal expected that a visit from my grandfather would mean that he would be able to tell him about my destructive behavior, and perhaps, be able to show himself merciful in my grandfather's eyes, forgiving the unforgivable. I think he wanted my grandfather to feel in his debt, so he could redeem that debt if the day came he needed to do so. But my grandfather never did what was expected. He had other plans. I stood outside the closed office door, listening clearly to my grandfather scolding the principal for having allowed me to be abused by other students. He accused him of incompetence, and told him in no uncertain terms that the protection of his students should be at the top of the list of duties he had to perform. He said he expected immediate improvements or he would be forced to report him to the Council of State. Leaving the principal in shock, he told me to pack my things and took me home. A few days later I was sent to a different Beca called Máximo Gómez, in honor of the Dominican general that fought in the Cuban War of Independence. That new Beca was much nicer. The buildings were well-built and painted, and there was a pool on the grounds. They had room for playing sports and they had a well-kept garden. The food was substantially better, as were the teachers and the fields where we worked every afternoon. This time there was no subterfuge. I was introduced as Che Guevara's nephew. The principal met me at the entrance and told me not to hesitate to tell him if I had any problems. I was given a very comfortable bed. My cousin Roberto, son of my Uncle Roberto, who was another of Che's brothers, also attended that school. He was older than I, and had talked to other students to warn them that I was coming and make it clear he didn't want me to have any bad experiences. Although I was not entirely comfortable in the role of protégé, it was comforting to have the protection of a cousin who often acted like an older brother.

Although I didn't experience any problems in that Beca, I wanted to live at home, in the hotel, in Havana. For the first time my fantasy was not to go back to my school and friends of Buenos Aires in my native Argentina, but to be among my friends at the Hotel, a place with which I was intimately familiar. My grandfather finally agreed to speak with the ICAP so that I would be allowed to leave the Beca and register in a public secondary school. I started my secondary training in a school nextdoor to the University of Havana, named Felipe Poey, after the Cuban intellectual of the nineteenth century. The entrance faced La Pera park, a lovely area of Havana amply shaded by beautiful trees. The walk from the hotel to the school was one a tourist would enjoy, passing by the University of Havana and the Napoleonic Museum.

I finished my seventh grade happy to be in that school. I made a very good friend named Carlitos Cecilia. Carlitos and I would run away from school on occasion to go his house and play a game of cards, or get something to eat while his parents weren't home. The doorkeeper at Felipe Poey school was my friend, because I brought him little ham sandwiches from the hotel every morning.

It was Carlitos that took me to my first boy-girl party, where I felt up a girl named Moraima. I was thrilled by the experience of my first touch of the female body.

About a month after school started I began cutting class to visit the Nuevo Vedado Zoo. It was a beautiful place where I felt the kind of peace I felt when riding a horse. Instead of walking to school, I began to take a bus directly to the zoo every morning. At that time there were still many animals left, and possibly more food available for them than for some Cuban citizens. I liked all the animals, but especially the cats, the elephants, and the monkeys. The elephants and the cats slept a lot, and it was difficult to picture them in the African jungle moving freely. But the chimpanzees seemed to have no idea they were imprisoned in a city, far away from their native land and their ancestors. Or perhaps they were simply determined to be happy regardless of their circumstances. They jumped from place to place playing, and as I watched I learned their caste system. A male chimpanzee who was a head taller than the others, was their chief. His name was Pancho. When the zoo filled with people, Pancho appeared nervous and somewhat agitated, and he screamed and hit the walls of his cage; He made sure the rest of his tribe went inside their constructed dwellings. Then he would start throwing excrement at the visitors with the ease of a practiced baseball pitcher. The more I saw Pancho, the less I liked this theater. In the mornings, when all was quiet, I had seen him as a competent leader dealing with the youngsters with tenderness and almost a perceptible good humor. The rest of the time he liked to peel and eat oranges and engage in grooming behaviors with the others.

There was also a small ape that always looked my way when I approached with a few crackers and nuts but would not come near me like the others. I started to make an effort to make sure some of the food reached him. One day when I approached the cage, the little one ran to the fence, stretched out his arm and offered me an orange. He wanted to be my friend. From that day on, even though I didn't eat the orange, I touched his hand and then I gave him crackers. I never knew if the little chimpanzee was male or female, smart or not, pretty, or ugly, but what mattered was that we became inseparable friends during those months. His handler didn't allow anyone but me to approach the cage. One day the handler asked why I didn't go to school. I told him that my teacher was sick. He never asked again, but as I left each day he would say: "I hope your teacher recovers soon!" Back at the hotel, I led a normal life. I left my books on the kitchen table as if I had been studying, changed clothes, and joined my friends in play. But at the zoo, the day came when I was no longer sure whether it was the monkey or I who belonged behind bars. Soon after, the school administration became tired of sending letters to my house that I intercepted, and they sent the school secretary to the hotel. My mother was terribly upset and told me I would have to repeat the year if I was unable to catch up all of the work I missed. But shortly after that the hotel began a major remodel and we were sent to live in Alamar, a worker's model neighborhood, and my father's choice of where we were to live. I had to change schools, and in those days there were no computers to keep track of a student's performance. My father wanted us to grow up as members of a society of laborers. Few laborers want their children to live that life, much less risk their own lives so that their children can pursue that lifestyle with pride. But my father's hard work and self-sacrifice would put the best laborers to shame. So one day, inevitably, a representative of the ICAP arrived in his Volga to take us to our new place in Alamar.

What a stark contrast there was to be between the luxury of the Hilton and the new home that awaited us!

The driver helped us out of the car and escorted us to a building. He said: "Here is your new home. It is furnished and everything you need is here. If you find that you need anything else, we are at your service."

I saw my room, the view from the balcony, the furniture, and couldn't muster a smile. It was as if Fidel had grown tired of our presence since the day we were welcomed at the Havana airport like important new members of the country.

It had been three and a half years since we arrived at the Hilton. The hotel had marked a boundary between reality and our seemingly impenetrable bubble. It had once been home to Fidel and my uncle and of other Commanders in the early days of revolutionary triumph. Leaving it felt wrong. I walked around for days haunted by a thought. *Was I really was Che's nephew? And if so, why have I been expelled from the Hotel to find myself in this neighborhood instead of in the neighborhood of Miramar where my uncle had lived?* I had a monkey friend jailed behind the railings of a cage in the zoo, my father's letters, my grandmother from Burgos, and a new apartment seemingly conceived in an aesthetic desert. The time for proletarization had arrived.

Chapter Eighteen

The political climate in Argentina had worsened. The army's coup d'état intended to rescue the country's destiny from what they perceived as anarchy, was soon followed by the formation of a military junta called the Junta Militar de Gobierno. Regardless of what their objective had been, the result of the takeover was to restore order by terrorizing the population. When I found out, I began to write my father compulsively. My mother told me that he could not receive so many letters, but when my head hit the pillow at bedtime and I went over the day in my mind, regardless of what a good day I may have had, darkness and silence spurred my mind to my father's lonely cell in a political climate that had increased the brutality of his jailers. My father was moved from prison to prison for a time, he contracted hepatitis, endured the merciless Argentinian cold weather in the South without even a sweater, and suffered hunger and thirst all because he had tried to help a friend inside the prison. In recurring thoughts I would say to him:

"*Papi*, come here!" and I would rescue him by taking his hand and leading him down a hallway that led to a room with a door to freedom. It was a fantasy that sometimes allowed me to give in to sleep. At times I woke in the middle of the night caught between my dreams and nightmares from which I emerged exhausted and often in mid asthma attack. At Alamar we were given two apartments in separate buildings in Zone Six. I am not sure how it was decided that I was to live with my mother on the fourth floor and my brother and sister were to stay with my grandmother. Each apartment had two bedrooms. The furniture was simple but practical. Each had a refrigerator, a television, a radio, bedding, pots and pans, and cleaning supplies, all provided for us by the State. Everything in the apartments was ugly. It seemed that in communist countries there was a department named The Department of Aesthetic Control, to make sure that nothing was attractive enough to give one pleasure. Even so, I felt somewhat embarrassed because Cubans had to give up what little they had to share with us foreigners. In my new home I learned about the CDR, The Comité de Defensa Revolucionaria. From the beginning of the Revolution, these committees had been established in every block of every neighborhood in the country to keep an eye on possible anti-Castro activity. But they also became places of malicious gossip and of domestic espionage, of Cubans being spied on by their own countrymen. It was up to the inhabitants of the house designated as a CDR to know the comings and goings of the neighbors on their block, what music they listened to, how they behaved. These things were reported to authorities, and also sometimes discussed in weekly CDR meetings. "Comrades, today we are going to read and analyze a speech by our Maximum Leader about the dangers of the Aedes Aegypti mosquito. Is everyone in agreement?" After all the neighbors raised their hand in agreement, propelled by a part of their brain previously unused before the Revolution, the meeting began in semi-darkness and the only sounds heard were the words of the speaker repeating the speech everyone had already heard, and the occasional sound of a mosquito flying past our ears. At first I felt strange in the new neighborhood and the new apartment, very aware of the significant difference between our luxuries at the hotel and the modesty around me. I was also aware that I was living with people who belonged to a much lower class. I was dreading the thought of changing schools and having to make friends again. Soon I realized that in order to survive I had to let go of all I had known and learn how to deal with my new situation. But there was one thing I held on to. One thing that I could not let go of: my father's imprisonment and the Cuban government's inability or refusal to help free him, despite his being the brother of Fidel's late and supposed-best friend.

My uncle Roberto joined us in Alamar after he was also relocated. He was the only brother my father had left. He looked a lot like him and they had been born on the same day some years apart. He did not remotely resemble a revolutionary like his brother Che, nor did he have my father's vehement temperament. He was a man who thought things out carefully, who possessed a good measure of courage; he was a good listener who took his time before expressing an opinion, a virtue practically absent from the Guevara family. Perhaps that helped to make him an excellent lawyer. Roberto was my gregarious uncle who loved the art of conversation. But something had changed.

Roberto was now in exile in Cuba and he had separated from my aunt Minusha. His current girlfriend was more fitting to the new era, more proletariat. Yet shortly after arriving at Alamar, he heard the call of the West. To counteract the weight of his lineage and the Revolution, he left Cuba for Paris by direct flight. His new daughter was born there.

I started eighth grade in a secondary school located a block away from my building. I made friends with some of my classmates as well as with some young residents of my building.

There were no more dichotomies between the hotel and the city, but only our new neighborhood, once the pride of the new society where Fidel took his guests to show them the accomplishments of equality in the Revolution, but now in disrepair, suffering from institutional disinterest. One highlight of the new neighborhood was the music. In the evening some neighbors got together to play Cuban music and to dance as the sun set. The music made me forget the lack of beauty in my apartment, and lightened my spirit, making homework a lot more palatable. Many of the musicians and dancers were black. I learned that not one black person from Patagonia to Alaska was the descendant of exiles. All of them were descendants of people who were taken to America by force, and who stayed there for generations working, many times under terrible and abusive circumstances while being treated with less regard than animals. I learned their stories from them, without the ideological confusion of textbooks. No matter how hard I tried, I had trouble imagining the instantaneous change their lives had suffered in Africa, the arduous travels to America to arrive in a land of terror, pain and humiliation, without the faintest hope of escape or of regaining their status as a human being. Despite their history, they did manage to escape sometimes through rebellion, but even when their bodies were in captivity they were freed by their music. That beautiful and infectious music they brought with them, reminiscent of their care-free and happy days in their beloved Africa. My mother returned to work two years after we moved to Alamar, but at the other end of Havana, in Miramar. Each morning she had to make a long trip, and after a short time she was offered a stay near her job from Monday through Friday. She worked for an association of Argentinians in exile, and participated in many activities, and for the first time in a long time, she seemed to leave her depression behind.

I tried to avoid her on weekends when she came home, not only because I had come to appreciate my solitude, but because she took every opportunity to call me into her bedroom where she would tell me how much I was like my father, and how despite the fact that he had proven to be a brave man, he had treated her very badly and left her alone in a foreign country to raise her children. Her words and the heat of the apartment mixed together into a terrible tension that sometimes made me think of squeezing her breasts or of finding myself trapped between her legs. I became angry with myself for feeling these forbidden feelings, with her for inviting me into her room, and with my father for abandoning her and putting me in a position of substituting for him. When my mother left, sometimes for weeks, I felt calmer and she seemed happier. Her job appeared to be a blessing for us both. I received a letter from my father shortly after one of my mother's visits home. We had been talking about music recently in our letters and he mentioned to me that besides the Rock and Roll I loved, I should listen to one of his favorite musicians, Silvio Rodríguez. He mentioned a song by Silvio, his favorite spmg. I found it and memorized it because it made me feel close to him. Lately I had heard rumors that Cuba was full of political prisoners like my father. Although in those years it was not easy to know that for sure, and our indoctrination did not allow us to recognize the barbaric excesses of the Revolution, there were hints that the rumor might be true. I think deep down, none of us wanted to believe it. Yet around us, in every neighborhood, when someone was a little too "different," whether because they were critical of the government or simply eccentric, they were ostracized and ended up in exile, or perhaps a Cuban prison. Eventually we found out the rumors were true. Dissention was becoming more visible. In 1980, a group of people took over a city bus and crashed it into the entrance of the Peruvian embassy where they asked for asylum. The official version said that the now-refugees had been heavily armed and that they had shot back when those guarding the embassy opened fire, killing a guard named Pedro Ortiz Cabrera The version outside of Cuba was that the occupants of the bus were not armed, but that Ortiz Cabrera had been killed by friendly fire during the attempt to stop the occupants of the bus from reaching possible asylum. I found it hard to believe that a group of Cubans anxious for shelter in the embassy would try to enter it by force, given the obvious desperation in the act of crashing through the gate seeking protection in the first place. The Cuban authorities requested the asylum seekers be returned to them. Peruvian authorities refused. Fidel publically stated that anyone who wanted to leave Cuba could go to the Peruvian embassy. Before long, bus after bus began arriving at the Peruvian embassy and it was ill-prepared for the onslaught. A few days later, Fidel recanted the invitation, but by then the crowd inside the Peruvian embassy numbered more than ten thousand people: men, women and children. People had come from all over the island for an opportunity to flee the glorious Revolution.

Fidel organized a parade of Cubans to repudiate the newly exiled. Buses were sent to schools and work places to pick up adults and children who were expected to attend a "spontaneous manifestation," and for a few days and nights, people marched in front of the embassy shouting insults that left those inside the embassy completely unaffected. I was one of the students selected to participate in that march, and after a short time of watching the overt hatred, of seeing protestors throwing objects at those crowded inside, and hearing their screams when the objects hit their target, I had enough. I told my teacher that I was going to my grandfather Ernesto's house three blocks from the collective madness I was trapped in. I arrived at his house and told him what was happening. I drank two glasses of cold water and went to the second-floor terrace, where I helped myself to a mango I picked from a fruit-laden tree growing adjacent to the house. I sat in a corner of the balcony unable to erase from my mind the shameful act I had been forced to participate in. Across from me was my grandfather's study, where he was putting the finishing touches on his book, *My Son Che*. From my place on the terrace, I could see on his desk a copy of the book titled *History Will Absolve Me*, written by Fidel in 1953, where he espoused his solidarity with a restitution of democracy and social justice to his country. The warmth of the sun and the sweet juicy taste of the mango did not keep me from wondering if history would ever absolve him, if history would forget his betrayal.

Inside the embassy chaos reigned. Food trucks approached the building and the employees threw the food from the sidewalk, over the fence, to the embassy gardens. There, the strongest men who had fashioned weapons from anything they could find, took the best rations for themselves. They did not hesitate to beat up or hurt anyone who tried to pick up a box of food before they did. These people were few, but Fidel used their behavior to say that all the people inside the embassy were like them.

Ordinary people who had chosen to enter the embassy to realize their dream of freedom found it difficult to bear the crowding, the heat, the disorder, and the violence. It is said that women were raped inside the embassy and that they yelled to the guards outside for help, only to be insulted further or ignored. One day in my school, we heard the story of a man who had thrown out his Syndicate identification when he entered the embassy. He was overheard saying to the angry crowd: "Keep your identification from the Syndicate. I don't need it any more!" A few days later, unable to withstand the conditions inside the embassy, he was seen again, his eyes brimming with tears, searching the ground for his identification without which he would be unable to return to his home. Freedom's price was more than he was prepared to pay that day. After several days of harassment from their countrymen outside the embassy throwing stones at them and screaming obscenities morning, noon, and night, those inside the embassy found out that the Cuban authorities had decided to extend permission to leave the island to anyone without a felony record. Anyone, that is, except the first fourteen men who had forced their way into the embassy. They asked those taking refuge in the embassy to return home and await permissions that would be issued for them to leave Cuba by way of Peru. The number of people waiting for an opportunity to join those already in the embassy was such that attempts to break into other embassies began. Fidel and officials of the communist government decided to open the port of Mariel near Havana, and to allow North American yachts owned by Cuban exiles, their families, and friends, or by organizations that supported Cuban exiles, to come and pick up anyone who wanted to leave the country and go to Florida.

From that moment on, Cubans who requested permits to leave the country from the Cuban Ministry of the Interior were required to fill out paperwork specifying that they were either delinquents, homosexuals, prostitutes, or vagrants, in order to qualify for their ticket to freedom. Those who only wanted to be free, or that wanted to reunite with far away families, those who simply disagreed with the goals of the Revolution, were hesitant to make such statements. But declaring oneself a prostitute or a homosexual was the best way to access a new life full of opportunity and new dreams. Non-political prisoners serving time for minor infractions were given the choice to stay in prison or leave for Florida.

In a famous speech, Fidel praised the prisoners who refused to leave the island and instead chose to serve out their sentences in Cuba. He told the Cuban people that those men knew that the worst Cuban prison was better than life in the most imperialist country on earth. Fidel, an avid student of Machiavelli, had learned to be a master manipulator. Very likely, no one was prepared for the avalanche of people who crowded the Ministry of the Interior requesting permits. They arrived in Mariel from all over Cuba.

Our next-door neighbors in the building were from the province of Las Villas. For days, relatives began arriving at their home in Havana hoping to take advantage of the opportunity to leave the island. Those humble guajiros from the country, for whom the Revolution was purportedly fought, their calloused hands and arms scarred by their work in the fields, told the authorities that at night they wore nylon stockings, panties, and transformed themselves into attractive women. They would have transformed themselves into anything if it meant they could escape from the island.

When the day came that they were granted their permit someone reported the event to the CDR. Soon after, a crowd of neighbors led by the president of the building's CDR were waiting for them as they stepped out of their apartment. The CDR-led neighbors screamed at the family with a rabid anger accusing them of being homosexuals, anti-revolutionaries, and whores. I watched from across the street where a group of us had gathered to listen to music, and saw the panicked faces of the children that until the day before had been playing outside the building with their friends protected by the same CDR that now led the senseless attack.

The crowd became louder. As the family neared the sidewalk their neighbors began hitting them at first open-handed and then close-fisted. Then a policeman who lived in the building approached and hit one of the guajiros in the head with a heavy rubber stick. The man's wife, unable to take the abuse any longer, began to shriek. Some children watching the spectacle nearby looked terrified. I crossed the street and grabbed a little girl's hand and told her to look into my eyes and nowhere else. I tried to calm her. At that moment, a young man who had been watching from across the street approached the angry crowd. He was over six feet tall. Either because of his height or because of the authority of his voice or both, he was able to get their attention. "All of you stop this!! Can't you see that the children are scared?"

The family took advantage of the distraction and ran up the stairs to the relative safety of their apartment. Only then did I let go of the hand of the little girl who was still wearing her Pioneer uniform, and who every day stood in her schoolyard and swore: "I will be like Che!"

For four days the soon-to-be-exiled family stayed in their apartment with their doors and windows closed. The angry neighbors continued their harassment, throwing eggs on their balcony and yelling insults. On the day that the patrol came to escort them to the yacht that would take them to their new country, they walked down the stairway to the patrol car following one of the agents. The patrolmen did not make an effort to protect them, but instead allowed the angry neighbors to beat up the family and spit on them. It would be their last memory of a neighborhood where they had lived for years, and of the people they had once considered friends, all because they had made the subversive decision to attempt to make a life in another country.

My neighbor's experience was not unique. Incidents like these occurred all over the island. In my school, two teachers who had applied for permits were escorted from the building and beaten, insulted, and spit upon all the way to the bus stop. The look in my teacher's eyes every time he was slapped, or spit upon, the look of incomprehension, fear, and an inexplicable hint of compassion, is still fixed in my memory. There were many serious incidents in Alamar. So much drama, and so much tragedy in the days of Mariel that never made the news!

Statistics were not kept about these incidents in Cuba. There was no free press, no press at all to keep the community informed. But everyone who lived in Cuba during that time cannot deny the abuses they witnessed. It happened everywhere that people were beaten, spit upon, insulted, as if it was some sort of general catharsis, as if they were exacting punishment of those who dared to do what most desired: go North. When the number of people leaving Cuban shores approximated one hundred and twenty-five thousand people, the United States asked the Cuban government to stop the emigration of its citizens. Many of us thought at the time that the majority of people who wanted to leave had done so.

It is true that there were delinquents among the crowds that arrived in Miami, and more than twenty five hundred newly arrived Cubans were immediately arrested there. But the great majority of new exiles were decent hard workers. They were a contingent of people who had once been enamored of the Revolution. They had participated in it, and at one time had been communists or communist sympathizers. Many had identified themselves as such for fear of reprisals, but some had served in the militia. They had been the enemies of the Miami exiles, the enemies of those who had now become their rescuers. For those in Cuba, it became clear that given the amount of people who had left the country, something wasn't working as planned. The Revolution suddenly found itself bathed in an unexpected reality. The old mirror had cracked.

Chapter Nineteen

A group of boys I listened to music with sitting across from our building almost every day talked me into going with them to a dentist's office near our school to steal Alginate, a material used to make dental impressions. Instead of saying no I gave them one excuse after the other, but part of me wanted to place myself in danger, to take some risks, perhaps thinking that behaving that way would make me feel closer to my father and my uncle but also suspecting that participating with the rest of the boys in this endeavor would ensure my acceptance into the group of my new friends. Eventually they accepted my refusal to help them steal the material, but they asked if I would at least serve as a lookout for them. I agreed. We were all adolescents and the consequences of being caught stealing by the Cuban police didn't worry us. But the older kids to whom we gave the material in exchange for cigarettes were fully aware of what getting caught would mean. Luckily the operation went as planned. I stood guard outside the building smoking my cigarette and looking as if I was waiting for someone to join me. Soon my friends were back and they thanked me for my help. One day on my way back from school, I saw a crowd and some policemen standing together in front of my building I noticed the majority of the kids were the ones that I had accompanied to the dentist's office a few days before. They were waiting for me to arrive. The police escorted us to the waiting cars and took us to the station in Guanabo. We had been accused of sabotage, and the police were surprised to see that we were just kids stealing in exchange for cigarettes. My mother arrived at the police station shortly after I did, arguing that I had fallen victim to bad influences in our neighborhood. She said this in front of my new friends and their parents. I felt embarrassed by her words to the core of my being, more so than for having been caught and detained. Thanks to my being a foreigner in Cuba and thanks to the fact that I was Uncle Che's nephew, everyone was freed. My friends' parents seemed caught between feeling offended by my mother's words, and feeling grateful to her for their sons' freedom.

The first time I lost consciousness after drinking alcohol, I had consumed a large part of a bottle of Rum at the house of one of my school friends. His parents were out of town. From the very first taste I knew that alcohol fit me like a glove. It seemed to meet every need of my young spirit. I was hooked. I began to get drunk with my friends in the afternoons. One day my friend Pedrín took me home. Almost as soon as I crossed the threshold, I vomited. Vomiting relieved my stomach but it did nothing for my severe headache the day after, nor did it stop a disconcerting dizziness and vertigo. I hid the truth from my mother who made it easy for me because she didn't ask many questions. In a way, I began to feel a certain pleasure in lying to her. During that time, I lied all the time. I lied about cutting classes, about smoking, about doing homework, about the company I kept. I also hid my frequent masturbation. Lying became the rule, my new and constant habit. From the time I was little, I learned from my family that a lie should never be told with the expectation that it would be believed. Its function was to appear indisputable by creating a kind of virtual reality for the listener, telling a story that was the total opposite of what actually occurred. My mother said I was good for nothing, that my father, the man who had betrayed her, was a million times better than me. She wondered out loud why he had left her alone to raise me. I wanted to know the answer to that question myself.

During this time I wrote my father more often. Sometimes he didn't answer my letters because he was being punished. The mail wouldn't reach him and his outbound mail was put on hold.

I don't know if my parent's separation or my father's request to be treated like everyone else was responsible, but I began to perceive that we were no longer so important to the authorities in Cuba. There were fewer visits from and little communication with the Council of State unless a problem arose that needed immediate attention. But we were always invited to any function that involved my uncle Che. I worried what life would be like for us the day that our relationship to the myth became unimportant to the Cuban government.

I was invited to attend an event in honor of my Uncle Che on the occasion of the anniversary of his death along with my relatives. Raúl Castro was the speaker. He told us how much my uncle meant to him and spoke of the pain his loss had caused him. He spoke of how he had been personally affected by his death and how his loss had also been a universal loss. Then he began to ramble on in an insipid discourse totally devoid of authenticity, destroying a tribute that had begun so well. He was not the orator that his brother and commandant was. Seated on the first row, I fell asleep and began to snore as my head bobbed towards my cousin's shoulder seated on the chair to my side. Raúl paused for a moment and my cousin elbowed me and woke me. I straightened in my chair and said rather loudly: "Is the bonehead finished?" My comment embarrassed many members of my family, but some of my younger cousins couldn't help but laugh. I was secretly glad to have been included in Raúl's invitation, which for a time quelled my fears of having been forgotten. My attendance in school improved due to two of my teachers. My literature teacher would forget all about the textbook and get carried away by literature itself, launching into brilliant monologues. The classroom became an oasis of pleasure and I was inspired to befriend my books once again. I particularly enjoyed his classes about Vietnamese poetry and the care with which a young man should pursue a relationship with a girl in that exotic far-away place of indomitable Indochina.

The other man responsible for the improvement of my attendance was my Marxist-Leninist Philosophy teacher. Usually teachers of this subject, which was taught beginning in the eighth grade, told the students what was expected, gave them a reading assignment, and went out to smoke in the hallway. We were taught concrete dates of historically significant mythical accomplishments of the Left. Most of the content was rhetoric and indoctrination. Passing the class required a forceful condemnation of capitalism and a fervent adherence to communism. But my professor was different. He was passionate about his subject and enjoyed teaching us.

I spoke privately with my professor about my interest in the Polish Solidarity movement. One particular morning, we began a conversation about the worker's strikes in Gdansk. We didn't talk in private as we had done before when I visited his office to learn as much as I could, and sometimes to argue fiercely for my own point of view. As we were talking Genoveva, the principal of the school, overheard us from the hallway just as I was insisting that there had never been an exit of more than a million people from a capitalist country. She entered the classroom and gave me a look I was becoming used to. She looked like a dragon breathing fire. But it was the coldness in her eyes when she shifted her glance to my teacher that made me feel as if my veins had turned to ice.

A few days passed and I did not see my teacher. We were told he had been transferred to another school, but no one knew which school exactly. I felt his loss keenly. A few weeks later, I called my cousin Ernestico, Che's son, to make a date to ride horses with him at his farm. He told me that Aleida had given the farm back to the State. I felt a mixture of satisfaction and disappointment. On the one hand, I knew that my uncle would not have accepted the gift of the farm to begin with and that he would have been glad of its return. On the other hand, I loved to ride with my cousin and I would miss those times we shared together.

I found another place to ride called Escaleras de Jaruco, where I had to pay five dollars an hour for the privilege. It was a fenced area in the center of a beautiful green valley, but I missed the Arabian horses I was used to riding on the farm. Still, I enjoyed the view of the verdant valley and the feel of the tropical breeze on my face.

I was my aunt Aleida's favorite nephew, but she never acted as if she was terribly glad to see me. One day she told me that my father was the only Guevara that was welcome in that house, because he was the only revolutionary in the family. Aleida had an aversion for the family of her dead husband. She had been a clandestine soldier who had lived in grave danger of capture or death during the Revolution. She resented the fact that her dead husband's family was not more active in government or in the propagation of the Revolution around the world. She and the children also had orders, as did all the families of higher-ups in the new Cuban society, to socialize only with others like them. It was a tight circle that seemed to reproduce the oligarchy's behavior of frequenting country clubs attended only by other members of their social class. They behaved in the same way as

Shadow of a Myth

those they had worked so hard to expel. My cousin Ernestico was the only one who was friends with people outside his circle, displaying a rebellious attitude almost never found in people of the ruling class. A rebellious attitude that would one day earn him a trip to Russia for a major attitude adjustment.

Not long after Aleida sold the farm, I began to date my first serious girlfriend. Her name was Yamilé. We became sexually active and saw each other as often as we could. I was a member of the first generation that had broken with the old sexual taboos of the other Cuba where virginity was as precious as gold. Perhaps the absence of religion, of bourgeois ethics, or the excess of free time or the absence of material incentives, favored the fall of moral barriers and social conventions. Now it seemed we lived in an island where free love reigned, tropical style. Yamilé and I were together for about four months, until when upon her return from a family trip to another province she informed me that she had made love to a much older man while she was away. I didn't ask for details, but it became clear that our relationship was over. I wasn't so much in pain over losing her as I was angry that she had cheated on me. A short time later, a mutual friend told me that Yamilé and her whole family had left for the United States. Suddenly I became aware that I could clearly hear the beating of my heart. I felt as if I were standing at the edge of a precipice. Although the United States was only ninety miles away, I knew that it would be impossible for me to follow her there. Yamilé had left her month-old puppy, Patty, with me. After Cocó in my early childhood, she was my main confidante, a twin soul like the chimpanzee at the zoo. The day after John Lennon died, my friend Jesús and I got together to listen to Band of Gypsies, a Jimmy Hendricks song. Jesús rolled a joint. I was surprised once I smoked it and realized that all it did was make me laugh and enjoy the music much more than usual. I wondered why this drug whose effect was much milder than that of a glass of rum, was so strictly forbidden. I understood that a drug that encouraged relaxation and laughter would probably undermine the speed in the assembly lines of the country's factories. But I saw marihuana and tranquilizers as drugs that offered a new dimension to reality. They helped people to access an entrance to the psyche through doors that normally remained hermetically sealed.

Hendrick's recording seemed to last much longer than usual. Smoking in silence between one musical note and the next on the guitar, I was caught up in a new-found subversive and pleasurable act. Jesús warned me to be very careful of getting caught with marihuana on my person. People were serving five-year sentences in prison for being caught with one marihuana joint. He cautioned me not to talk about the experience with anyone, no matter how much I trusted them.

Why did the men who ruled the island, so full of moral defects and so eager to turn in friends and families to the authorities in terrible acts of betrayal, condemn the use of a harmless weed? I immediately swept the floor, then mopped it, to make sure there was no trace of ashes to be found. Jesús watched me, indulging in uncontrollable laughter. Euphoria didn't help me to forget, but instead it helped me to reminisce. I much preferred my rum and other liquid spirits. The Beca had already taught me that I did not want to be enclosed in a cell full of delinquents for a year, never mind five. I didn't want to take any chances and smoking the coveted weed became a thing of the past. Pedro Miguel, who liked to be called Peter, was my neighbor and my classmate. He was from Oriente province, from the city of Puerto Padre. We liked to listen to music together. He left school to study military engineering and for the first two years he lived at school. When he came home on weekends we would argue about the military. I thought that being a soldier meant, in fact, to be a murderer of multitudes. I reminded him that it was the opposite of what our favorite rock singers advocated. He always told me that someone had to show up when it was time to defend one's country. Peter told me that he had gone to a military university because his grades weren't good enough to allow him to follow his dream of becoming a civil engineer. But he told me not to worry because he would always feel the same as always about following a path of peace. A few weeks later, I waited for Peter to get home and when he did we walked to the Malecón. We sat together on the wall with the ocean lapping the rocks behind us. He said he had something to tell me. He looked sad and worried. "Martín, in the last few weeks they started training us in earnest. I was sent to La Cabaña. At first they explained how the firing squad works. They told us that only criminals who had committed brutal acts like murder and rape were killed. A few days later, they took us to watch a live demonstration. They explained to us that only two of the guns are loaded, and the rest are blanks. That way no one knows who is responsible for the death. If these people are deserving of punishment, why do they keep the soldiers from knowing they are the executioners? Martín, I have now witnessed several of these, and I am terrified that one day I will be asked to be part of a squad." Jesús covered his face.

At first I tried to get him to meet my gaze, but soon I fell in the same abysmal space he inhabited and not only did I understand why he covered his eyes, but I wished that I would never have to see his eyes again. The silence between us grew and I could think of nothing to say. I wanted to run away but couldn't. The face of terror I had glimpsed was replaced by an intense cold shaft inside me, accompanied by the desire that Peter would suddenly and quietly disappear. But Peter was my friend who needed me more than I had ever needed a friend, and I stayed beside him. I asked him: "Peter, what does it feel like to kill a man?"

I signed up to go to East Germany with two of my friends. Our plan was that once there we would escape to West Germany. I had no desire for the things that capitalism could give me, but I was thirsty for freedom of expression and freedom of movement. I had gotten through several steps in the process before my application was abruptly rejected.

Another way of leaving the country would have been to sign up as an international combatant when I turned eighteen. I must have been desperate to leave because I tried to exercise that option twice. Once I signed up to go to Angola as a laborer apprentice, and another time I signed up to go to Argentina as a guerrilla fighter. In order to accomplish my goal I would have to undergo intensive military and political training. The first part of my training would be completed on the island. The second part in a third-world country in any conflict where Cuban troops were involved.

When I made inquiries, I thought that if I went to Argentina, I might be some use to my father, whether helping him to liberate the country from the dictatorship that held him prisoner, or helping him escape as I did in my nightmarish dreams.

I began suffering severe stomach-aches at all hours, every time I thought that the moment when the authorities would take my candidacy seriously and would call me to serve. I had nightmares every single night, until someone in the America Department ordered my mother to dissuade me of my ideas because my father had left orders that we were not to leave Cuba. I was instantly overcome by a feeling of relief and felt the protection of my father, albeit retrospectively.

Chapter Twenty

I took every opportunity to travel inside Cuba with my cousins and my friends. The desire to travel was intense, but I couldn't go back to my country, and we didn't have so much money that we could permit ourselves the luxury of a vacation overseas. Twice a year I went camping with my cousins or close friends to an area in the north of the island called Puerto Escondido. Two beaches of white sand surrounded by a barrier reef made Puerto Escondido a treat for the senses. We always camped in the same place facing the ocean to the left of one of the two sand beaches. From our camping spot we had a marvelous view of the white sand and the very blue ocean. We had met Nuñez Jiménez, a man who had been one of the Commandants in the Sierra Maestra and was now the preeminent archeologist and anthropologist of Cuba. His house in the suburb of Miramar in Havana was next door to my Grandfather Ernesto's house, and I had met his daughters. Núñez, his cooks and his guards were higher up on the beach. They had several good-sized tents and even a generator that allowed them to enjoy their air conditioning. Still, it was uncommon for someone who could have stayed in the penthouse of a high- class hotel, to choose instead to commune with nature in this way.

A few hours after we arrived we noticed that Nuñez Jiménez camp had grown, as several more tents had been added. There was a visible increase in security. We learned that Raúl Castro, Fidel's brother, had arrived. After we secured our tents, Raúl's bodyguard walked to our camp. He told us that if we needed food or water we should feel free to go to their camp and ask for them. We told him that we ate what we fished but that we might take them up on their offer of water.

Late in the afternoon we stopped by the camp and I went to say hello to Núñez. Raúl was seated on a canvas folding-chair. He said hello to my cousins with whom he was already familiar. He asked me who my father was. I told him I was Juan Martín's son and asked him the same question I had asked Fidel years earlier. He ignored the question. He told his nephew to join us if he liked, but he refused. We left the camp and went swimming until the late afternoon, when we spotted a caguama, a large sea turtle, far from the shore. We decided that the sea turtle would make an excellent dinner, and very carefully, trying not to attract the attention of our fellow campers, we killed the turtle and began carrying it in pieces to our campground. Unbeknown to us, Raúl's nephew who had refused to join us earlier, had been watching us. He approached us and said that the cook would be happy to help us cook the caguama.

That night all of us had a veritable feast in Raúl's tent. Raul said to me:

"Are you the one who fell asleep during my speech in honor of your uncle's death? I remember that you wouldn't stop snoring and your cousin had to wake you up to stop you from mak-

Shadow of a Myth

ing noise?" "Yes," I said, and laughed nervously." "I remember how startled you were when your cousin woke you!" He laughed. I couldn't believe that someone like him would remember the embarrassing episode so many years later.

I found that I liked Raúl. He seemed less terrible than his reputation among the people. Many saw him as much more cruel than his brother Fidel. He also had a reputation for being a frequent and happy drunk despite being the leader of the Cuban Army. My uncle had been a good friend of Raúl's during the Revolution and during the establishment of the new government. Although it is hard to believe that someone so close to Fidel could be totally innocent of wrongdoing, I think that he appeared to be much different than his brother. He carved his own niche as army leader and he ran the army effectively. The one thing he never did was challenge his brother.

I returned home after a very pleasant trip to find my mother in the apartment, very upset. She told me my father had gone missing. She confessed that no one knew where he was, that every trace of him had disappeared on the day he was transferred to another prison. I feared the worst, but I was not prepared to internalize the possibility that my father was dead. I decided to only think about that possibility at bedtime, when I couldn't help the wanderings of my mind.

The mystery lasted only a few days, but in those few days I made some irreversible changes. I began to drink every single day of the week. I stopped attending school. I looked for work as the janitor of a company in Guanabacoa.

Alcohol allowed me to replace a more absurd reality. In an attempt to straighten out my life, I became a volunteer at the International Camp of Pioneros during my time off from work. Unfortunately, the attempt to take my life in a new direction was sabotaged by my behavior, when one night a friend and I left the students alone while we spent the night with a couple of female instructors. When we woke up we had an urgent message to go to the director's office immediately and both of us were summarily dismissed.

I went back to our apartment to find my mother in a very good mood. She appeared to be as happy as possible given the circumstances. She had just returned from a trip to Mexico to learn that we would be moving to Miramar. The Council of State had agreed to her relocation so that she could be closer to her work and where we could all live together.

Alamar ended for me that week, as its reputation of a model proletariat neighborhood also ended as it gave way to the decay so prevalent in Cuban society. I had spent five years in Alamar, and I didn't abandon the place completely. Sometimes I went back to visit my friends, but I never regretted my change of circumstances. I had missed my old way of life. I made friends in Alamar but hardly a day went by that I didn't feel a profound weight in my chest that almost kept me from breathing. Addiction had found me in Alamar, and I continued indulging myself hoping that someday I would be able to find my way to clarity again.

Our new home was on the corner of First Avenue and Sixteenth Street. Our apartment was large, larger than three units in Alamar put together. It had two living rooms, a large kitchen, and several bedrooms and baths. We were also given the apartment across from ours that had an ocean view for us to use as storage, or to house our invited guests.

Miramar was one of the most beautiful neighborhoods in Havana, and many of the most powerful made their homes there. Many embassies were located there, along wide avenues adorned with palm trees.

We were given new IDs that identified us as foreign technicians and allowed us to shop in stores that catered only to visiting or resident Russians, and to use the pools and bars of the Sierra Maestra building that housed the Soviet guests who enjoyed their rations of ham, Vodka, and cold Pilsner and Urquell beers brought to them directly from behind the Iron Curtain. At the Sierra Maestra I met people from Hungary, Czechoslovakia, and befriended some Russians my age. They taught me to play chess. Their parents played to pass the time. Curiously, these people who were no fans of bathing, spent long hours in the pool playing chess in the water. They stood a little higher than waist deep in water, as if they were trying to make sure that their underarms would have to wait for their weekly baths to get clean.

My mother had been promoted in her job and was now in charge of a magazine for Argentinians in exile. My relationship with her had become very difficult. We argued about everything at all hours. I had given up hope that I would ever be cherished as a valuable human being capable of accomplishing anything worthwhile. We argued loudly over the most inane subjects. The most minor problem turned into yelling matches between us. I was embarrassed to be so grown up and to continue yearning for her love. I felt weak. I told myself that at my age my uncle had been much more of a man than I was. That thought would inevitably send me in the direction of my next drink.

In truth, I had become an alcoholic. My life no longer made sense, even to myself. My Aunt Celia had been living in Switzerland. She traveled to Cuba around this time and in a moment of clarity I confided in her about my need to drink. She made an appointment for me with a psychiatrist friend of hers before returning to Switzerland. I never went to see him. She found out and wrote me a very severe letter, but she didn't completely close her door to me.

After moving to Miramar I was closer to my friend Evelio's house and we picked up our friendship as if we had never been apart. Evelio loved to go camping as much as I did, and he also shared my habit of drinking and smoking. Our frequent get-togethers brought us even closer. Shortly after one of our trips, our family was summoned to the Council of State.

I felt apprehensive on the way there. All of us were quiet when we arrived, filled with dread and hope. We learned my father was about to be freed. We learned that the woman with whom he was living when he was apprehended would also be released. I became aware of a feeling of pain inside me, but before it could take me over the thought of my father being free again filled me with joy. I began to fantasize about the day we would get the call that he was free. Would I hear the sound of his knuckles knocking on the door or would I be the one waiting at the door of his prison? Or perhaps I would receive a letter from him telling me that he was out of prison and couldn't wait to see me? In any case I imagined that I would hug him, preparing myself mentally for that moment. But I had been eleven then. At twenty, perhaps I should curb my enthusiasm. The love of a child that spends years waiting for his father is a love that remains child-like, not in its innocence but in its fragility, in its weakness, in the way it is expressed with tears and a sprinkle of sighs.

Until the moment he was freed, his letters were a balm to my heart. Sometime they were like a map of how to approach my life, how to maintain a positive attitude in a world full of challenges. In some cases his letters were nostalgic, referring not to the times we had shared together, but to the years of his childhood and adolescence. Reading my father's letters, I felt him close. He kept me company. I thought if he was given the choice again to leave or stay in Cuba he would have chosen to stay. But I had known from the time I heard the news of his imminent release that my father had no intention of participating in a family

Shadow of a Myth

reunion. As soon as I learned that he had been released, I wrote him a letter. I asked him when I would hear him knock at the door. Two weeks later, I received his response telling me that it was still not a good idea for us to travel to Argentina. That I was a man now and I should understand that things are not always the way one wishes they were. Poor man, I thought sarcastically, all those years inside fearful cells and now that he could enjoy his children, they talked about hanging on to him tightly with their need for his warmth—a need that would again impede his freedom. Poor man, I thought seriously, poor man who could treat his own blood that way. He must be going through something very difficult, bleeding from a wound in his soul so deep it was impossible to imagine. I went to a bar alone. The influence of my uncle's absent presence was on my mind. I might not have grown up to be like Che as I had vowed every morning in the schoolyard, yet he had shaped my life in so many ways. I thought about the contrast between Fidel and Che, thinking I much preferred my Uncle. The one thing I liked about Fidel was his aversion for anything that looked like work. There was nothing in him of the laborer.

Uncle Che was fully committed to living his life as an example to others of the hard work required to forge a new revolutionary society. He volunteered daily to do manual labor and would work morning-to-night alongside the people with great fervor. Because Che worked so hard, the other leaders of the Revolutionary government could do no less. Fidel went to work reluctantly while my uncle was alive, but as soon as Uncle Che left the country he stopped going, and in my remaining years in Cuba I only saw him once, in a documentary, with a hard hat, surrounded by body guards, not working but eating with the workers. I would prefer that to the almost religious fervor that drove my uncle to spend hours every day working the fields.

My cousin Juan Ramón studied accounting, my cousin Rosario studied physics in the USSR. My cousin Pedro was becoming an architect and my cousin Roberto studied economics. My cousin Rafael was in medical school. I had opted to study my career in the university of the streets. Raymond Carver said that drinking is an act that takes much time and dedication. I was learning how right he was.

Chapter Twenty-One

My father was released from prison in March of 1983. He had been in jail for eight and a half years. Although a military government was in power in Argentina, it had been weakened in the war against the Malvinas Islands to the point that its end seemed near. My father chose Buenos Aires to live a life of "freedom," while being closely monitored by the government.

My mother busied herself preparing our return to Argentina. My dog Patty was the only obstacle to my return. My friends of a lifetime, my girlfriends, my lovers, the laughter and rum in the Malecon, I could keep alive in my thoughts and through frequent correspondence with my friends. I spent the months prior to our move to Argentina getting in trouble. No sooner did I get out of one mess that I was involved in another.

I was sick of the constant mention of Uncle Che. Quite frequently I felt watched by critical eyes. It seemed that even the things I did well were insufficient to compete with the totem he had become. Ignoring what the authorities thought of my behavior I wasn't ashamed of my anti-social attitudes. My visits to jail for minor or medium infractions ended the moment my uncle's name was mentioned. I felt aligned to the ghost of my uncle when I was able to go against convention or to upset anyone in authority.

I stayed entrapped in that rebellious state much longer than was appropriate. Finally the time came for us to leave for Argentina. I was at once fearful and excited. I wanted to immerse myself in the culture of the country I had yearned for so many years, to taste the tastes and smell the smells I had missed. And I wanted to see my father's face, to hear his stories from his lips and to tell him mine, to talk with him about every subject under the sun. I wouldn't ask him anything. Not even if his obsession with following in his brother's footsteps had been worth the cost. I wasn't looking forward to saying good-bye to my friends. But I went to my friend Lily's house, visited with my friend Ana María, and spent a few hours with my friends Evelio and El Nene. I walked in the sand near the shore and took time to say good-bye to the sea, accompanied by my dog Patty and an almost empty bottle of my favorite rum. I wondered how my brother and sister were feeling about the reunion. It had been a long time since we had shared our thoughts unhindered by my drunkenness.

The next day we landed in Argentina. When we entered the terminal building, my father was waiting for us leaning on a low wall that separated the passengers from those waiting. I forgot everything and everyone around me and began to walk towards him using all my energy to keep the child in me from running into his arms. My father's smile welcomed me as did the warmth of his embrace, and for a moment I felt whole.

After ten years of absence from Argentina, I was overcome by the familiar smells and textures of my childhood and experienced great pleasure seeing my country again and at the same time great sadness, feeling the city more alien to me than Havana except for the smell of Milanesas in Buenos Aires and the smell of the entrance to the metro, the "subte." It seemed those scents had been stored inside my nose all the years I was away.

My father lived with Viviana, the woman he was seeing at the time he was jailed. She was a member of his political party and like him had spent eight and a half years in prison. For the first few months my brother and I lived with my father and Viviana in their small apartment. The initial dislike I felt for Viviana was reciprocal. My father had warned us against returning to Argentina and now his motive became clear.

I started to work along side my father and for the first time I began to enjoy working and developed respect for the productive life. My father and I started a contracting business with four other political prisoners that had been released with him. I had so much fun that each night I went to bed with my stomach aching from the laughter we had shared. Later we began to promote Cuban culture selling imported books and music in audio and video format.

I stopped drinking for two years, was about to enroll in school again, was working with my father, feeling very well and living in an attractive room where I spent much time reading Shakespeare translated to Spanish. I was the happiest and most peaceful I had ever been. Even so, I decided to return to Cuba to prove I could live up to expectations.

Some long twelve years before, I had arrived in Cuba, a prepubescent child. In those years, I had done all I could to remain a child before being given back my father and my country, my extended family of origin, and a saner life. I wanted to close my eyes and come awake in the middle of a field with my friends Silvina and Juan Martín, returning to the carefree times of our childhood, suffering from terminal amnesia.

Finally, one day I accepted that despite all my efforts I could not stop time, and before I forever lost the synapses in my brain that made it possible to cross the street, button my shirt, and tie my shoes, something in me decided to allow the storm I had been avoiding to flood my whole existence. I surrendered to pubescence and adolescence with intense vigor, given the intense resistance I had mustered earlier. I felt like an Olympic runner racing without the benefit of a warm-up. In my way, I became a fan of antisocial attitudes and disdained social graces, not unlike my uncle Che.

Thus, I followed the footsteps of my heroic uncle, feeling in this both pride and humiliation. He contaminated everything that existed around me. He took my father to a prison where he felt more pride than in the presence of his children, he sent my mother to a bed where she cried her tango tears with the help of Diazepam, led all my cousins to scream "if I had balls I would be like Che!" and he led me to escape from his shadow helter-skelter, when the straight-and-narrow path became impossible for me to travel. Compulsivity did not work with me. They had cocooned me in it during my childhood.

I stopped playing board games, garden games, sports; I stopped enjoying my own company. I had become a good-looking teenager who could provoke intense desire, and I had also been consumed by that desire. I hungered for human flesh—the flesh of any and all women, but most of all the flesh of women easily led to bed, women who, like those in my dream, would walk me to a field, show me their breasts, and let me rub myself on them.

Feeding my appetites only made them stronger. There was no ugly woman prior to possession. I wasn't sure whether I was making love to them or to myself, or if maybe between us we were making love to a third person twice my age. Young whores,

Shadow of a Myth

pink-veined boys, voluptuous adolescent girls. I observed myself in my dreams like an eternal voyeur.

I woke to sensual pleasures fully but filled with angst at seeing myself so lacking in my mother's eyes, in the eyes of those who visited our house, my schoolmates and the girls in my neighborhood. Adolescence was like a cape that covered me with originality and protected me from my most intense fears. I rehearsed several personas without taking permanent residence in any of them.

I avoided growing up in the absent presence of my imprisoned and almost martyred father, in the absence of a beard, and despite having achieved my uncle's exact height when he became a phenomenon and began to forge what would become the platform for the myth in the midst of his own doubts and fears. I began to hide behind the veil of drink, to enjoy the recesses of desperation.

My father's letters stuck to my being as closely as my uncle's rifle stuck to his and the dreams of imitating the courage of their father stuck to his children. I escaped into my books. Reading allowed me to sprout wings and fly away from the constant hyper-vigilance I felt. Salgari, Verne, Dumas, and Pushkin opened the way, but Herman Hesse's *Steppenwolf* pierced my brain until it found lodging in my consciousness.

I tried to absorb some Revolutionary enthusiasm, something of that flame that seemed unable to light my heart, my loner soul, or my skin, not being one attracted to sterile sacrifice. I began irreversibly toasting my skin in the Caribbean sun and almost imperceptibly one day found myself dancing a kind of Guaguancó suited to my bones that filled me with plasticity and rhythm.

Making new friends, I basked in my anti-social behavior. In that role I was able to feel the virility necessary to continue to grow in some direction. My uncle and my father had swallowed up my potency, as I became conscious of the excesses committed in the sacred name of the Revolution.

I opened my mind to the words of the Cuban elders about the story of the Cuba they remembered, and mentally observed the heroic Che become a boring bureaucratic Minister, a Minister who lacked creativity, who felt death in the midst of security and the fire of life on the edge of a blade, while his counterparts ate Bulgarian chicken and drank rum telling tales of their Revolutionary prowess. They had become censors of any attitude that disagreed with their stomachs.

Observing the privileges enjoyed by the creators of equality, I lost respect for them and became aware of an attitude of repulsion inside me, a mild spark of conscience, that made me proud of the path of controversy and doubt that I had chosen. I was experiencing antipathy for the Revolution, not only for strictly political reasons, but also for aesthetic ones. I had every intention of leaving power and the future to the same band of imbeciles that hugged an hour after a goal, or in the case of Cuba, a home run.

I aspired to become the stereotypical image of the Cuban man: a good friend, a joker, a drinker, a risk-taker, a lover, and a man of grace. But I felt far from the ideal Cuban in the company of the meekness demanded by the regime, a meekness exhibited by most Cubans once known for their rebellious character.

It was then that Rock and Roll became my favorite form of expression. I wanted to feel like a young Englishman, rebelling against something important.

I wanted to walk the streets of London, to try drugs and to question the value of society in general, as well as to question my Cuban society, not the earlier Cuban or the earlier Argentinian consumer society that I no longer remembered. I thought what Cuban society needed was to be plugged in to an electrical outlet at which point every citizen would howl until the sun and electrical sparks became one. Perhaps the electrical charge would jolt them out of their meekness and bring back the memory of the rebels they had once been. At that time I didn't know that thousands of Cubans had opposed the system I lived in, a system now full of a strange mixture of adoration and terror in the presence of Fidel. Back then Cuban citizens had confronted him directly, not in the way of my adolescent games. I did not embrace confrontation nor did I embrace a particular political position.

I had expressed my opinion that territorial armies were useless and that those pursuing a military career were in the business of perfecting criminality.

After witnessing Lech Walesa's worker's movement in Poland, I referred to the communist block as the oppressor of the masses—a continuation of Imperialism in a territory ruled by vulgarity. I had publicly stated that Fidel exhibited an innate adversity to truth, that almost all of the high government officials lied about how they really felt about equality, that everything was staged, and that the efforts of the Revolution to duplicate itself in countries like my Argentina had been a frightening exercise of power.

In an effort to escape that reality, I advocated that we should make love night and day, drink rum, and even smoke pot, although smoking pot was punishable by many years in a Cuban prison. We should live life to the fullest, listen to Rock and Roll, anything that would help lift our mood a little. But despite my bravado, I discovered a profound discomfort in my spirit when I spent time alone. It was only in the company of others while pretending to be a prototype of frivolity that I found solace from that overwhelming feeling that threatened to swallow my soul into its darkness.

I arrived at adulthood without the size of my penis growing nearly so much as I bragged that it had, and unable to make my muscles as strong as implied by the anecdotes I recounted. My eyes could not locate the horizon of my path. I couldn't see where I was heading. The only compass I had been given was rigged in such a way that true North was never an option.

I had lived and worked alongside my father in Argentina after many years of yearning for his presence. I knew another life, other ways to express rebellion. I had run far away from Che and read Shakespeare, Joyce, Borges, and Carpentier. Despite the peace I found in Argentina, now I was returning to Cuba to show that I could be as good as anyone and that I had left my rebellion behind me.

My intentions lasted as long as it took the airplane to lift off from Argentina and land at Jose Martí airport. I had found my way back inside the mouth of the wolf. Not Fidel's, not Che's, but the mouth of my own deformed creature and its insatiable hunger to eat its young, I being the first it chose to devour. Back in Havana, I met with José Millar Barruecos, Fidel's personal assistant who was also known as Chomi. He was in charge of the Council of State. It was made clear to me that I could come back but I would not be able to go to school like my brother and sister. Instead I would be required to work. I would not be given a stipend like my brother and sister received.

I have to admit that what I wanted to do when I returned to Cuba was to go to the university and major in psychology or sociology, so I was disappointed. I started working at Ediciones Cubanas and the work was based on pure lies. Everything, absolutely everything, was staged to appear as if work was being accomplished. I was in a department that received magazines from around the world and we delivered them to the highest authorities of the politburo, the army, and the ministries. There were abundant publications full of sensationalism. I had always associated the reading of such magazines with ignorance.

Cuba was going through a crisis of confidence in every sector of society. Critical voices began to be heard speaking with the ease, intelligence, and brilliance that the courage of telling the truth brings. Magazines arrived from Moscow with news that deviated from the classic-comic-book flavor of the communist press. Something was changing. People joked in the streets that the only truthful information that appeared in *Granma*, the official Cuban Communist Party paper, was the date, and sometimes the weather forecast.

I went to live with a girlfriend named Ana. Her parents were living in Switzerland because her father was the Cuban ambassador there. After a week at Ana's house, her mother arrived from Helvetia to end the audacity of her daughter and her boyfriend living together. After serious differences between Ana's mother and me surfaced, I moved to the office of a Peronista political party in Cuba. She said that all blacks were delinquents. This was a popular view of almost all the leaders of the revolution, a peculiar way of understanding racial equality.

After a time working at Ediciones Cubanas, I stopped going to work to dedicate myself to attending alternative Rock concerts, poetry readings, gatherings of painters and concerts of the "*Nueva Trova*," a style of music that developed after the Revolution.

At a concert, I met Mariana and started a relationship with her in which I spilled all my anger and angst and all the frustration I carried within me, as well as the joy of life, the restless spirit. She was the best person I met in those years and one of the gravest errors she committed was to believe me when I told her each day that beginning on Monday of the next week I would change. With her I displayed the ability to be despicable, a person even I despised. There was a lot of love between us. In my sense of it all, she loved me and was good to me, but I didn't take care of that love as I should have.

My grandfather Ernesto complained that I didn't go to visit him until three months after my arrival in Havana. It was true. I was resentful because he had been opposed to my return to the island. My cousins, with the exception of Ernesto, had totally distanced themselves from me. Repression had increased in the two years I had been absent from the island. There was intolerance to Rock and Roll concerts, and intolerance towards those who resisted becoming part of conventional life.

With Mariana, Evelio and other friends I went from the jazz festival to the festival at Varadero, to the Rock concerts, and to parties at the home of friends who harbored ideas of freedom. In reality my generation was showing signs of going crazy from being choked by the inability to read anything but that which was prescribed, to have an opinion, to speak freely, or to find a way for artistic expression and political dialog outside the very restricted parameters imposed by the authorities.

People from the Council of State were sent to my home at different times of day to tell me that if I didn't conform, I would be sent back to Argentina, until one day they asked me to go to a meeting in the offices of the Plaza of the Revolution.

At that meeting they expressed their worry about my behavior. They needed to mold me to their ideals or banish me because as Che's nephew I was supposed to be an example to those around me. What they didn't say was that the example they wanted was the example of submission—the kind of submission displayed by every member of my family in exchange for a few crumbs of the existing corruption.

Chapter Twenty-Two

I had resumed my life in Havana with no help from the Council of State or from my family. The only place that I could find to stay was the apartment in Alamar that we had once used for storage. This time, my dog Patty wasn't with me. The friend who promised to care for her in my absence told me she had run away. I hoped she hadn't run away to try to find me and talk to me about her feelings of betrayal when I left her behind.

This time, something unexpected happened. I heard about and observed an authentic characteristic of the socialist government with which every Cuban, Russian, Polish, or Czechoslovakian citizen was familiar with to a greater or lesser degree depending on their perceived danger to society; the eye of the all-seeing "big brother." I had heard of it, but I had never experienced it myself.

From the time I was fired from my job when I was a diver for the Baconao Turquino Project, I had felt paranoid. The paranoia, I suspected, was partly related to the quantity of my alcohol consumption, but also to a few incidents that taken together seemed ominous. The feeling grew one day when I arrived home to find a letter someone had slid under my front door while I was gone. It was a letter summoning me to a meeting at the Council of State building with Fidel's secretary Chomi. It warned that it would be in my best interest to attend this meeting to "keep things from deteriorating further." I didn't know what to do and decided to telephone Chomi's office to tell him I was ill. His secretary answered the phone and greeted my explanation with a long silence. She told me it was hard to believe that I was not well. She put me on hold, and when she picked up the phone again, she proceeded to recite in great detail the places I had frequented in the past two weeks. The Hotel Bellamar in Varadero, the bars of Twenty Third Avenue, the UPEC and the UNEAC buildings. She also mentioned everyone who I had been with or spoken to.

I bristled at the thought of having been so observed. From the Committee of the Defense of the Revolution, breeder of spies in every block of every neighborhood, to friends and girlfriends who were being paid to keep an eye on me and report weekly on my activities, I was now a victim of "spy mania." I had personal knowledge of what others had spoken of for so many years. I had known of famous people who visited the island and were filmed in compromising situations as insurance, in case they ever decided to denounce the government or the system. But why me? The only thing that set me apart from anyone else was my relationship to Che. Why follow me? What possible danger could I represent? I now understood the truth of a popular saying in Cuba: *Outside of the island a paranoid person is someone who thinks they are being followed. In Cuba, the man free of that perception is not sane, but irresponsible.*

Havana was living through a time of transition. In the USSR, Gorbachev had taken power. An ex-agent of the KGB and its former director, he had executed as many enemies of his Bolshevik country as he was ordered to execute. But he had recently spoken of wanting to bring economic and political reform to his country, and that affected all of the Soviet satellite countries, including Cuba.

Suddenly all things Russian became more popular. The magazine *Novedades de Moscú* (*Latest News from Moscow*) now arrived on the stands without the ideological diatribe it was once known for. Little by little, a new style of writing, devoid of the old preaching style, opened a curtain that gave us a different view of our up-to-now familiar Soviet neighbor's house. The house was a larger house than ours, but it was laid out the same way.

There was subtle and careful criticism directed at the years of Soviet supremacy. Back in 1957 Sputnik had been propaganda for the Soviet Union, but now articles were being written that addressed scientific discoveries and other articles discussed issues of daily life. Articles dealing with anthropology were still sprinkled by the usual exhortations about the virtues of socialism, but were not as alienating as they had once been. Magazines were filled with the subtle color of change and at times referenced cultural changes. By seven in the morning, the stands were empty of the new publications. People shared them freely. The foreign technicians, mostly Soviet, began packing their bags to go back to the land of Pushkin and Semionov. The winds of change could be felt everywhere.

Everywhere except inside the island, that is, where the winds of change did not blow at all. On the contrary, we felt as if we were breathing toxic air. We were being warned that if for any reason we had to confront Imperialism without the support of those who had helped us until then, we would not forget the failure of their revolutionary promise, but we would do what was necessary to stand in our own version of Cuban Stalinism. Thankfully, we would still have access to rum and condoms.

I heard that my cousin Aleida, Che's daughter, was getting married. I would have paid little attention had the news not been accompanied by a rumor that upset me: I was to be excluded from the celebration.

I told my girlfriend Mariana that it wouldn't bother me if my cousin Aleida, whom we affectionately referred to as Aliusha, didn't invite me, since we saw each other only "every time a bishop died"—another way of indicating the infrequency of our contact. What bothered me was that I was being warned not to go—not by my cousin, but by the Council of State. A mutual friend who at that time was the girlfriend of my Uncle Che's son Camilo, Aliusha's brother, told Mariana and me that she was going to the wedding and had been told Fidel would be there and there would be tight security. I called another one of my cousins and asked him if he thought that I should attend without an invitation. He said he had been asked to tell me not to go.

I wasn't sure if the Commandant was upset with me or if it was Aleida who didn't want me there. I wondered if perhaps she was worried for the guests that I was going to deprive them of a third of their portions, since there are few things I like more than a party where good food and beverages are served. Mariana stared at me sweetly with her eyelids at half-mast, a look that I knew held a reproach: "¡Martín, coño! Every day partying with Evelio and your other friends and when there is something special we could enjoy together you're forbidden to attend!" I felt fangs replacing her usual tenderness and tolerance, fangs that dug deep into my throat.

I glanced at my Tag Hauer watch. I had made off with it during my diving days before I was judged in front of an assembly of my peers and asked to leave. Looking at it made me remember that day, the day when it was determined that this Indian no longer belonged to that tribe—at least not to the floating tribe on the south of the island. I told Alejandra that we should sell the watch. It was submersible up to two hundred meters and quite valuable. Then we could go to the UPEC and have a few Chakatas before the Council caught up with me and made me go work somewhere else.

The words of Lázaro Ponce de Leon still echoed in my ears. He was the captain of my ship and an official of MININT. "I gave my life to the Revolution. All you have ever done is take advantage of it!" The Revolution had taken almost everything from me. I was fighting to keep it from taking the little dignity I had left. But I turned and walked out of his life without an argument. I decided to sell the damned watch.

My uncle Che thought that the genetic memory of the predator that lived within a man, the predator that went after his neighbor's sustenance, could be eradicated in one generation, or in two. He thought this could be accomplished by a conscious ideological discipline that would wash away old capitalist vices through the education of the people. The new man, the seed of future generations, would become the envy of all men in the world, of all those who lived in "dog-eat-dog" societies.

These new generations raised in solidarity, part of the international proletariat, taught to motivate themselves morally to become better workers, would live in an iron-clad revolutionary discipline and would understand the just punishment dealt to anyone who deviated from the revolutionary ideal. They would be men of moral rectitude and exemplary conduct.

It was there in my view where the failure of this idea, not a totally erroneous one, lay. I too thought that man was a product of his education and that it was logical that if one was raised not to feel a need for unbridled consumerism, one could live without it. We could, for example, have a couple of brands of each product which should be sufficient for each of us to be content in life without forcing all of us to have the same. I was someone who didn't need much. I would have been happy with a good couch, a nice living area, good food, something good to drink, maybe a car, a small boat, and the right to do what I wanted so long as I didn't violate the rights of others.

But what kept me from embracing the idea of a new society was no doubt the uniformity of thought demanded of the youth in the country and the strict order, the quasi-religious morality, the oppression against those who for whatever reason were not ready or willing to belong to that new army.

I was struck by the contradiction of that idea and the fact that I knew Che had been raised by people who respected one's right to rebel, by a mother who broke social conventions, and that he was someone whose parents had encouraged questioning everything—including questioning the norm.

I felt that my uncle, wherever he was, was telling me:

"Martín, I had good intentions. This wasn't an impulsive thought, but a beginning of a chain that one day would lead to a society that could replace capitalism, the exploitation of man by man, not through a violent revolution, but by the invitation of workers of good will everywhere who could present a model that would seduce much more than the thought of personal gain. But you, nephew, son of Juan Martín, of the always-distracted and sweet Patatín, don't dismay. Don't become anyone's vassal or follow me in my mistakes. These projects are not for you, even if they were for Patatín. I want you to be free. And this, whether freedom means that you will live a life of excess, whether you will be brave or a coward, sane or a little perturbed. Faced with the mire that my ideas have been turned into, you have my permission to fight against them or not. Don't lose heart and don't give in. This thing you're living in was not my dream."

I began to listen to a cassette tape, my favorite. I listened to it every morning, ballads of the Rolling Stones, Deep Purple, Led Zeppelin, and Grand Funk. I went into the bathroom with every

Shadow of a Myth

intention of bathing but when I turned on the shower I was greeted with the sound of dry air. No water. I took the pail to the back terrace where the metal tank was and filled it. I heated a pan of water and mixed it with the water from the pail and invited Mariana to join me. There was no water left in the tank. We bathed to the music of Memory Motel and then I splashed a little Brut 33 that I seldom used dreading the day it would run out. I picked up the few coins I had left, made sure I had my passport, and we went downstairs after making sure no one was on the other side of the door or waiting for us on the stairwell. We walked to the bus stop and got on the bus headed to El Vedado, thankful that we had seats for the long ride and hoping that no pregnant women or old ladies would board and force me to be a gentleman.

The bus rode down Via Blanca, paralleling the green of the grass, the black coral reef, and the blue of the sea for a few kilometers until it approached the Almendares tunnel. It was a pleasure to ride the bus through those streets whether I was sitting or standing squeezed among others like a sardine in a can. The tunnel was a legacy of the Batista regime, one of the last construction projects he oversaw. It travels under the bay and joins Old Havana with East Havana continuing its trajectory bordering the ocean by the Malecón. The bus wound its way through the old city and climbed Twenty-Third Avenue crossing the heart of El Vedado, one of the nerve centers of Havana. The trajectory ended at Avenue G, also known as the Avenue of the Presidents.

We arrived at a meeting of the UPEC, the union of Cuban journalists. The meeting took place in a splendid building of the old Cuban bourgeoisie. The side terrace had been converted into a comfortable bar shaded by rich vegetation. Mariana sat down and asked for two Chakatas, a drink made from tea, rum, ice, and lemon. Tea had become popular in Havana and it was in vogue to drink Chakatas in the bars that had become known for their iced tea. Shortly after we sat down, Julito, a journalist who was discontent with the regime and was not always careful about expressing his views, joined us.

Mariana wasn't very interested in discussing politics. Evelio joined us and we drank another Chakata. I kissed Mariana and excused myself, asking her to wait for me. I told her I would be gone about an hour and a half. I was going to sell the watch and later I would go to a store to buy sandals or jeans for a friend and make some money. I asked Julito to keep an eye on her while I was gone.

Evelio and I walked out into the heat and humidity of the city with a little rum in our bodies. The sun on my face gave me a hallucinogenic aura and I enjoyed the walk down the avenue to the Malecón.

We looked for a cab on the street corners, stopped some and asked the drivers where they were going. We couldn't find one that would take us where we wanted to go to until we told a driver we were headed to the center of Havana and we would give him five pesos above his fare. He told us to get in. We arrived at Papito's solar, or tenement building, which was in the neighborhood of Cayo Hueso, near Trillo Park, a park with abundant trees and known as a place where one could get marihuana. The majestic trees could not hide its state of decay.

I paid the taxicab driver and asked him to wait for us while we ran a few errands. I told him to either keep the meter running or tell me how much his time was worth. He said he would charge us thirty pesos and we readily agreed, knowing the difficulty of finding a cab in Havana that was going to where one needed it to go.

I asked Papito if he would buy my watch. He told me the watch was great but he was no diver and was even too old to swim in the Malecón. I said:

"Why aren't there any black divers? Are they afraid of sharks?"

"No", he said, "the reason blacks don't dive with tanks is that if the frontier guards saw a black diver under the water they would arrest him for illegally trying to flee the country."

We laughed and joked for a while. He gave me three hundred dollars for the watch, about half of what it was worth, and said he would wear it for a few days to get the attention of girls from outside of the neighborhood, who might have money to buy a watch, or until he found a diver that would be willing to buy it.

Papito was a good man. Although he was in business to make money and not to dispense charity, most of the time he made his friends good deals. He invited us to drink some of his homemade rum, a concoction that he made in a container where he slow-cooked fruits and rice. The beverage was called "Guarafina." Papito had the money to buy any rum that could be bought with Cuban pesos, but he was a colorful character who loved his Guarafina as much as the best rum that could be purchased, and liked treating his friends to a beverage made by his own hands. In that way he honored his friends.

Before he went into business buying and selling goods and solving problems in his neighborhood, Papito had been a professor of philosophy at the University of Havana, where he had been dishonored for his strong disagreement with its philosophy. In the late '60s, he had participated in an effort to organize a group that would fight for the rights of blacks in Cuba—a kind of Cuban black-power movement. He was a prolific poet who had hundreds of poems and verses written on pieces of paper all over his house.

I told Papito our cab was waiting and he suggested I ask the driver to join us. Half an hour later Evelio, the cab driver, and I said goodbye to Papito. We'd had the opportunity to encourage some business between Papito and the cab driver that was going to get a pig for Papito from a farm outside Havana. Both would profit so we left more satisfied than when we arrived, warmed by the good conversation, the profitable business and the Guafarina. The Guafarina's bouquet could not compete with any rum, but at least it was strong and hit the stomach with the force of a thousand demons.

CHAPTER TWENTY-THREE

The cab driver had become our ally for the afternoon, a quasi-friend referred to as a *"socio"* in Cuba. He told us he was in the process of a divorce but had been unable to leave his house because it was impossible to find another one. This was an issue for many citizens. Housing was at a premium and it was as difficult to leave the house of one's parents, as it was to get divorced. Trading a house for two could mean landing in an undesirable neighborhood if one didn't belong to the high command. Many people opted for dividing the existing house into two smaller houses and when doing so was not possible, they resigned themselves to looking into the face of the new lover of the ex-wife, and to hear their laughter and other noises she and the lover made through the never-quite-closed doors of Havana.

We arrived at Carlito's place. The cab driver stayed downstairs smoking and listening to his radio and we went to the flat. The heat was unbearable and my shirt was open. When we passed by the door of the apartment before Carlitos', a mulatto girl who lived there stared at my chest. I looked at her and said:

"Inside my chest is a heart that can be yours when you wish."

She laughed and turned, making sure her skirt hiked up almost to her waist, allowing me to appreciate her intimate curves. She turned her head, smiled, and disappeared from view, leaving me breathless in a rush of arousal at her door. Evelio pulled me forward to our friends' house. A flight of fabric and Guafarina with ice: a Cuban rumba.

Carlitos invited us to sit for a while in his air conditioned apartment and offered us cold beer. He asked about Mariana and I told him she was waiting at the UPEC and told him we had a cab driver waiting downstairs. He gave me two hundred dollars and told me he needed a four-speed Phillips table fan, a blender, and a Casio watch and that I should spend the rest of the money on t-shirts and women's blouses and sandals. I looked at my watch and drank down my beer faster than I would have liked. I left Evelio and Carlitos in the apartment. I could hear my friends making fun of the way Mariana had me under her thumb.

On my way back to the street I looked for the mulatto girl, but she was nowhere in sight. I climbed into the Lada next to the cab driver. The driver wanted to know where we were headed and I told him to take me to the Seaman's Club next to the Castillo de la Fuerza. I asked him to leave the windows down, preferring the air of the Malecón to the air conditioning in the cab.

As we drove next to the Malecón I thought about Che riding through these streets years ago in his official car. He must have made this trip hundreds of times as a Minister. I imagined the first time he marched triumphantly into Havana with the rebel army a few days after Fidel. I had seen a picture of him accompanied by other soldiers. He rode a truck with his shirt open, holding his rifle, a cigar between his fingers, showing little affinity with bourgeoisie cleanliness—a trait we shared at that time.

I pictured him in the Malecón, a vision more unreal but pertinent at the same time. In a moment of rest he might have preferred to take a walk by himself, perhaps with his driver and a bodyguard. He would have stopped in front of the Dubill Hotel where the waves crash with force and elegance. He might have told the others that he would be done in a couple of minutes, that they should wait for him in the car.

I pictured him climbing the Malecón wall and sitting there like just another Cuban, a Cuban in love with the sea, his girl, the rhythm of the Cuban dance known as *"el son,"* and the sun. As a wave broke he might have been sprayed by the water and his face would have been cooled by the wind. He might have experienced a sensation of pleasure, of belonging in that instant in that place. For a moment he might have almost fused with the water and the stone of the ledge, but when the water began to recede he surely felt struck by a sensation that had overtaken him occasionally since his childhood. The sensation of not belonging in this or any other place in the world except in the arms of a woman with a voice that calmed him. He may have thought to himself: "What am I doing?" The image of his mother blending with the image of his lover must have flooded his vision now filled by doubt, and clarity would have followed.

The next wave, much bigger than the last, may have drenched his face and his chest. Like a wet cat he might have jumped backwards and told the driver and the bodyguard: "We can leave now."

I contemplated the pleasure I derived from the subterfuge of illegal activities; definitely the thrill was greater than the reward of money. It was my way of rebelling against the arbitrary and unjust laws imposed on the citizens of the island. The wind on my face and tousling my hair made me feel closer to the instant of clarity that follows doubt than to that victorious entry into the city, that magic moment of the hero, a fleeting but exuberant experience.

The cab driver parked near the Seaman's Club, a building with colonial walls across from the bay, and I asked the driver to wait for me a few buildings ahead. I bought everything Carlitos had asked for plus a couple of beers for the cab driver and myself. I descended on the elevator resembling a Caribbean Santa Claus and when I walked out on the street found police on both sides of the building asking passers by for their ID, a routine activity in Havana. The first store to sell merchandise from capitalist countries in Cuba using American dollars opened in 1976 in the Habana Libre Hotel. Shortly after others followed in Miramar, in the port of Havana, in Varadero, and in time, they also dotted the tourist hotels. The stores didn't have just tourist articles like soaps, perfumes, local artwork, t-shirts and hats bearing the logos of cities, beaches or product brands, but instead the shelves were filled with things useful to daily life. Things like electric appliances, casual attire, elegant clothing, sports clothing, the coveted blue jean, shoes, slippers, and food and drinks of much better quality and variety than those sold in stores to the citizens with ration cards. In those stores one could buy Cuban cigarettes without pieces of wood that impeded suction like those in packs of Populares and Aromas, the brands available to the Cuban people. The stores carried cigars of the very best quality. Eventually those were made in Cuba with tobacco from Vuelta Abajo, a zone where the most exclusive and refined tobacco leaves in the world grew. They stopped growing there when the owners became upset with the government due to their not following proper production standards. These stores had little to attract tourists. The buyer could think of nothing else but the desire of possessing those goods that were abundant in capitalist countries. Those products could only be bought in dollars and could only be bought by people who had been born anywhere but in Cuba. One could go into those stores with a passport from any country, or with a foreign ID. There were various categories of foreigners: permanent residents who had been in Cuba a long time or planned to live the rest of their lives on the island. They had rights that the rest of the people did not. They were able to travel to their countries of origin once every two years, paying for their tickets in pesos. They could also shop in certain stores. Then there were temporary residents, those who didn't know when they would leave the island. The majority of exiles belonged to that category and although they were allowed to shop in stores, it was understood that they didn't have money to do so often. Then again there were the foreign technicians, mostly from socialist countries of Eastern Europe, and mostly from the Soviet Union. They had the right to buy in special stores in Cuban pesos. These stores were only for them and were filled with better-quality products than those available to the general public, especially two products belonging to Cuban collective nostalgia, ham and apples. In addition, the technicians, who were less technicians than they were socialist, could buy merchandise in other stores. They were not controlled by national agents and they always had representatives from their countries of origin living in their midst. They lived in neighborhoods inhabited exclusively by foreign technicians, in Miramar, in a complex of buildings with pools and restaurants called Sierra Maestra, the thirty-story Foxa building in Vedado, and in a Russian neighborhood of quaint and colorful houses near Alamar with its own private beach.

The students comprised another group. The students were all those who were on the island only to pursue their studies. They couldn't work and they couldn't buy goods in tourist stores, although there were places where they could buy certain products in dollars. Most of these students came from third-world countries and were considered a low social class. They came from places like Angola, Mozambique, Ethiopia or Nicaragua. Nothing bothered a Russian more than to have to deal with a group of Nicaraguans or Angolans drinking in a bar that was meant only for them. In the entire island there was no underarm that stunk as much as the underarm of a Soviet citizen. Yet the Soviets said the Angolans were a dirty people and they avoided the Nicaraguans because they fought when they had too much to drink.

The second-most-privileged group was the diplomats. They had a life that required little sacrifice. They earned a hefty salary and were protected by diplomatic immunity. In stores where they could shop one could tell the difference in the quality of the merchandise. They were stocked with the very best that Cuba could offer. They were the sadly famous *"diplotiendas"* of Miramar and Siboney, the neighborhoods where the haute bourgeoisie lived before and after the Revolution. The difference between the diplomat shops and others was vast. The name *"diplostore"* or *"diplobeautyshop"* gave a place a reputation of excellence. There was a time when a beautiful girl was called a *"diplogirl."*

Lastly, there was a group of the truly privileged. A new kind of foreigner had begun to arrive in Cuba. They were the least loved but the most coveted. They were the businessmen who arrived with government approval. Spanish, French, Canadians, all dreaming of economic benefits but for some arbitrary reason, they were assimilated by the system as capitalists with a Revolutionary touch. They were the owners of hotel chains, communication enterprises, and oil companies, millionaires who opened businesses in Cuba without the worry of syndicates and free to hire workers who would never go on strike. They bought goods in any store they wanted without being bothered by any agent or any law in the books. They were the famous *"siemprebienvenidos"* — the "always welcomed."

Cuban citizens were considered the bottom rung of society. The natives of the country could not enter into any of the aforementioned stores nor could they touch foreign money. That is the truth, pure and simple. For years I had criticized those stores and the fact that anyone, regardless of their age or profession or their race, would find it reasonable that in their country beautiful and good things could only be bought by citizens from other countries and only with foreign money. I could find no Revolutionary reason to explain this. But I had learned a few years earlier to live in silent indignation, and although it's true that I was uncomfortable with the state of events, I didn't hesitate to use them in my favor. I became a conduit for such goods to reach the Cuban people—at a price.

I walked between the police officers that were hassling a young man who was waiting for someone to bring his purchase out of the store. I walked about ten meters when a loud voice stopped me: "Citizen, stop please!" I was asked for identification and I gave them my Argentinian passport. They asked me if I was a sailor. I knew I didn't look like a sailor or a tourist so I told them no, that I was a resident. They asked me to open my shopping bags and looked over the content of each. They said I had to go with them to the station.

I told them the fan was for my house and the blender also, and that the rest of the goods were presents for my family and my neighbors. I explained that my family sent me dollars frequently. They listened as they escorted me to the patrol car and invited me to climb in, and took me to the station around the corner from the Seaman's Club. We passed the cab that waited for me and I caught sight of the worried driver. He hadn't gotten paid yet.

In the station I was taken to a room with walls that hadn't been painted in a long time. I could smell the foulness of seldom-cleaned toilets. A policeman that had not been in the car that drove me to the station asked for my passport and told me to take out everything that was in my pockets. I put everything on the metal table. A pack of Partagas cigars, a lighter, various pieces of paper with telephone numbers written on them, three hundred dollars and a few quarters. They took my things and left me alone sitting on a desk in the room.

I looked around and realized it was an office that wasn't being used as one. There were three chairs on one side and on the other side there was a desk and a typewriter. There was no sign that the room was being used for anything other than interrogation. Two policemen who outranked the ones that left replaced them. They started asking me about my work, they asked why I had so much money and why I needed so many sandals and blouses of the same size. Their tone of voice and attitude changed when I repeated the same answers, that it was all for me and my friends and family, and that the dollars were sent to me by my family. They told me that it would be best for me if I told them who had asked me to buy those things. That if I refused to tell them I would be incarcerated. They reminded me they had prisons for foreigners. The highest-ranking official asked:

"Do you know karate?"

"No", I said, taken aback by the question, and added, "I learned judo a few years ago."

"But your knuckles look like those of someone who practices karate! You like to fight, right? You're brave? You want to fight me? Just you and me?"

I lowered my eyes. Looking at the other two would have meant a dare to fight alone. If I looked him in the eye with the little respect I felt for these brave men in uniform I was sure I would get hit immediately. I was forced to think fast. The comment about my knuckles had been an excuse to provoke me. My fingers were thin so my knuckles looked large for that reason. Their tone had become too threatening. I said:

"I don't know karate and I don't like to fight. I am between jobs right now. I don't know what my next job will be because the Council of State will assign it to me. The Council of State is in charge of me because I am part of Che's family which is why I don't look like a typical foreigner."

I didn't want to divulge my parentage because I didn't want Chomi, Fidel's secretary, to learn of my activities but the situation required me to take that risk.

The officers' faces took on a look of surprise. Their tone of voice and manners underwent a radical change. The aggressive official left the room and one of the others told me to be patient, that they would check my story because my passport did not identify me as a resident. I was left alone with only one officer who offered me some coffee. I asked him to bring me my cigars or at least a cigarette when he came back. When I was left alone, I could hear a man being beaten near the room where I was being held. It was obvious he had no relative in the spheres of power. An hour later, a high-ranking officer came into the room.

"Martín", he said, "you will leave here right now and we will take you back to where we picked you up. I'm sorry for the inconvenience but you live here and you know it is not usual for someone who doesn't work to have that kind of money and buy those things. That is why I recommend, between you and me, that whatever you are doing, you stop and get a decent job." He shook my hand and ordered I be taken back to the Seaman's Club. When I arrived there I saw the cab driver had left. I had to find another with bags in hand and my nerves on edge.

When I arrived at Carlitos' place, the cab driver was seated in the living room relaxing, waiting for me to pay him, having made himself at home. We laughed for a while as I told everyone the story of what happened. I finished the croquettes that no doubt had been fixed by Carlitos' mother, and had a couple of cold beers. Evelio reminded me that we needed to leave. Mariana had been waiting more than three hours in the UPEC. I said good-bye and went back to the UPEC, about four hundred meters away. The sun was starting to set and I walked through El Vedado saying hello to acquaintances, avoiding the deep holes in the sidewalk, contrasting the beauty of the homes built before the Revolution with the existing poverty made so real by the slow deterioration of those houses falling into ruin like old elephants that can no longer follow their pack. I walked through one of the few places in the world where one could witness decay that knew no shame.

The decay of the façades of buildings and houses, presented the reality of the misery of those residents who could no longer paint their houses occasionally, or buy new furniture, or replant a garden to improve the look of their home. The city made me think of older women past their prime, with rounded bellies, double chins, sagging breasts, whose eyes still hold the electricity of life in them. They have the energy of someone who believes that any day could be their last and can concoct a cocktail of pleasure much greater than young women with tight skin. After all, they possess the same skeleton, like painted buildings in contrast to the decaying structures of El Vedado.

The buildings of Old Havana, even though architecturally superior, didn't allow me the same imagination. Their decay was brutal. They were ruins that stank. In contrast, El Vedado continued to show good bone structure and was inhabited by people of some elegance.

Chapter Twenty-Four

Mariana had waited at the UPEC until an hour before I arrived. My friend told me that Mariana's girlfriend Jenny had picked her up to go shopping at the Habana Libre. I ordered a Chakata and went to the interior patio for a while thinking about Mariana. She was the perfect partner. She had left her studies at the university to walk with me on this steep path that had no visible goal.

The path was all. There was no project, plan, or illusion for us to hold on to. On this path there was only room for emotion and adrenaline and for exploring the question of whether there was any pride in total failure.

Every day I was grateful for Mariana's company, for being able to wake up with her face next to mine, but I chided myself for not keeping her safe from her desire to save this drowning man, to grind and refine the diamond. The diamond was already sold, and the drowning man was suffering from an incurable disease.

I went back to the bar and sat at a table with some journalists anticipating a stimulating conversation. Bruno, Julio, Danilo, Lissette, and I were there, and we all felt good in one another's company, sharing the first drinks of the evening. My friends had sharp and intrepid brains uninhibited by arrogance. Judging from the conversation I walked in on, they had already dispensed with the preliminary greetings and polite social conventions. They were discussing without much caution a subject that was prohibited in Cuba and in any Socialist country: the armed sector of the Revolutionary Party of the Workers, the ERP, a Trotskian Argentinian organization that had disappeared after the coup of 1976. They spoke about Leon, Trotsky, and Stalin, a little carried away by their enthusiasm, thinking that perhaps soon all journalists would be able to speak freely about this topic and every other. It was possible that in their fantasies they entertained the thought of publishing their ideas.

At that time dissidence did not take the form of wishing for the absolute substitution of power or the end of the Revolution. There were still men willing to try anything, who believed in the possibility of breathing new life into the existing regime, creating flexibility in government, humanizing the rigid hierarchy, and as a result, obtaining a more participatory society where everyday issues could be dealt with by the people, leaving the more transcendental issues to the party and its directive organs. Their goals weren't overly ambitious, but it was the hard-headedness of a government that chose not to grant the most minimal and innocent of freedoms to the Cuban people that led in time to the brutal repression of anyone who dared to even minimally express their disagreement with the powers that be.

The great majority of journalists were privy to more than half of the news that wasn't published, and suspected the other half, given the jealous way in which it were guarded. Many of them experienced severe frustration as the years passed. Every professional is aware of the ethics of his profession. Cuban journalists were no exception, and they had to live every day betraying their professional ethics, in almost all the news they reported. In some cases they began to exhibit mental disorders and self-esteem issues. Many were alcoholics. Some tried to find work in the sports section of newspapers, or the weather section, in a place where they didn't have to act like compulsive liars every day. The socialist press didn't give them an option of writing in the Society pages because, of course, they didn't exist.

The more daring among the journalists tried to find clever ways of disseminating classified information, risking censure. A few felt that they couldn't live with the constrictions and became part of what was considered the antisocial element. Some of them managed to leave the country and others left journalism for other professional careers or even menial jobs. A few ended up hanging themselves, and some went mad.

When journalists are criticized as the most deceptive of professionals one has to understand that they were under extreme pressure not felt in any other profession in Cuba, although professors, social scientists, philosophers and others were also victims of extreme control by the authorities. A doctor, for example, had less opportunity to lie than a journalist since a kidney stone and a sonogram didn't have the same danger of political subversion as that of any newscast.

"We have not reached our objectives of increasing crops this year even though it would have been easy to exceed them."

Or "Soviet forces invade the city of Kabul."

Or "Today is the twentieth anniversary of the summary judgments that led to the assassination of many and the unjust imprisonment of others." Or "An important member of the Party has been disgraced for having sexual relations with a minor and for having parties in his house which were attended by other high-level members of government."

Despite the fact that journalists were the biggest violators of their professional ethics, many of them were the bravest members of the opposition to the government, and in the last fifty years of the Revolution, they have been the founders and members of dissident groups even to the current day.

During all of my time in Cuba I didn't find one book, movie, or documentary, nor any newspaper article, that spoke about Leon Trotsky or his role in the Revolution of 1905 or 1917, his role in the leadership of the party in Leninism and later in the international opposition of Stalin's totalitarianism and his Communist Party that drowned a people in blood and terror. Not only could I find no information, I could not find any negative references to Trotsky except for a couple of chapters in a book about the October Revolution referencing his bitter betrayal by the proletariat.

In Cuba, the image of Stalin wasn't revered because in Russia he had criticized the cult of personality, the deification of someone still living, and it was implied that perhaps some excesses were committed during his time. Any criticism had to be viewed in light of the difficulty of the times in the only country that pretended to care about the happiness of the laborer and the farm worker, the USSR. At the time, the USSR fought an enemy that used unclear methods during times when definition was required and half measures were unacceptable.

While it is true that after the October crisis Fidel had never been one hundred percent enamored of the USSR, and my uncle Che before leaving the Ministry and dying in Bolivia had begun to see fissures in the moral integrity of some communist leaders, until Gorbachev stated in a discourse to the people that things would change in the satellite countries, there had never been a protest to any order that was issued by Moscow. Oil, guns, and grain trumped all the moral and ethics that had existed since the beginning of time.

Shadow of a Myth

We pondered the question of to what point it was forbidden to talk about Trotsky and Trotskyism because the Soviet Union had suggested it, in that particular way it had of sticking its nose in the internal politics of theoretically sovereign nations. Or if in truth it was the Cuban leadership who was responsible for forbidding any talk about him, as they didn't condemn Stalin's way of doing things, his use of complicated plots, defamation, imprisonment, and murder. Perhaps the Cuban government felt no antipathy for those arts.

I brought up the fact that Trotsky posed the idea of a permanent revolution, referring to the triumphant classes becoming the bourgeoisie and to the abandonment of their solidarity with the workers in the rest of the world, and then I lowered my voice and said, "We're sympathizing with a man that proposed permanent revolution and I wonder, don't we have enough with the eternal and omnipresent Fidel? Do we want a hard-headed Russian encouraging a constant battle against the bourgeoisie?" We laughed.

I paid my bill and when my friends saw how much money I pulled out of my wallet, Bruno asked if I had started working. I told him I hadn't, that work was alienating. I cited Paul Lafarge's theory, Karl Marx's son-in-law, in praise of leisure. My friend Pensotti wrote an essay about Lafarge's theory. Work, defined by Engels as the means of transformation from monkey to man, never played that role. It was leisure, earned by years of work that made possible the development of the brain, of communication, of the arts. A production line is the least ideal place for the promotion of creativity.

The word "work," according to Pensotti, held within it all perversions imaginable. The root of the Spanish word *"trabajo"* itself comes from the Late Latin *tripaliare*, a verb that means torture and is made up of the words *tres* and *palus*, the place where men were tied to be tortured.

I had a few last words with my friends and stepped through the door of that beautiful mansion into the Havana night. Two of those friends were later repudiated by the Cuban authorities and became exiles in the United States. Another was arrested for walking with a foreign tourist and having ten dollars in his pocket. The tourist was his girlfriend and today she is his wife. He spent ten days in jail being questioned. That man had taught people to read, and prior to becoming a journalist had been an agricultural engineer who had led several important projects in the course of his life. His career was over after those ten days, and he left the island forever to live in Argentina.

Every time I spoke about the superiority of the man who didn't work I felt good; in truth it was only because I liked going against convention. Not working wasn't good for me although the periods in which I didn't work were treasured interludes for the exercise of my brain, if not for the development of my creativity. The trouble was when I wasn't thinking, I drank. Then all the gray cells I accumulated with my thinking were atrophied by my excessive alcohol consumption.

Jenny lived in El Vedado in a sixteen-story building near G Avenue. From the sidewalk I could see the light was on in her balcony. The building was marketed to prosperous professionals in the years previous to 1959 and the arrival of the Revolution. Each apartment took up a complete floor. The quality of construction was superb and the elevators continued working like new after eighteen years without maintenance of any kind.

Mariana told me through the intercom that she would be right down. I spent at least fifteen minutes telling her what had happened and apologizing for being late, for drinking beer, rum, Chakatas, but at least I didn't have to apologize for spending all the money. She begged me not to spend all the money on drinks. After some time we rode the elevator to her friend's apartment.

Jenny lived with her brother and her very attractive mother. All of them were smart and cultured and it was a pleasure to end that night in their company. Jenny's mother was a TV personality who had her own show at that time on channel six.

I didn't want to be labeled everywhere I went and every once in a while I found places where I was comfortable listening instead of talking. They were places where I held back the arsenal of my criticisms taking into account that some people worked hard at making a living and that they should be allowed to do so with a certain dignity.

In Jenny's house I was treated with affection. I liked that she loved the icons of the Nueva Trova, the new Cuban music, and that she also enjoyed listening to Rock and Roll. Her brother had a very critical although somewhat innocent view of the government, and her mother was unhappy with the rigidity that was evident in Cuban radio and television. There was another reason why I felt comfortable at Jenny's house. Jenny and her family were relatives of another figure of the Revolution, the then-deceased president of Cuba, Osvaldo Dorticós Torrado, the man who had worn a suit at the fair where I had spoken to Fidel so many years before. He was Jenny's grandfather on her father's side. Her mother was related to Guillermo Alvarez Guedes, a comedian who had emigrated to the United States in the first years of the Revolution and who became famous in Miami. His comedy was heard in Cuba through the underground.

Eloísa, Jenny's grandmother, was a jovial woman and in addition, a beloved actress for the members of my generation, due to a famous series on TV where she shared the stage with Reynaldo Miravalles, an actor who was as famous as he was repugnant.

We discussed the matter of censure on Cuban television and the lack of independence that a producer or director was given. I glanced at Mariana, noticing her fine features, her rosy cheeks that looked like apples from Asturias as she enjoyed the company of her friend. Mariana had come to Cuba from Belgium where she had spent the first few years of political exile with her parents and her family. She belonged to a well-to-do family in Santiago de Chile, one of those very traditional Catholic families. She had lived real socialism and had the same old conflicts of whether to respect her parent's ideology or to trust what her own eyes revealed to her. That sophisticated girl was now my girlfriend, the woman I lived with, my guardian angel. I winked at her and gestured that I was ready to leave.

Jenny told me she would go to my cousin's wedding and said she would see me there. She knew my presence would not be welcome because she was my cousin Camilo's girlfriend. I seldom saw Camilo any more or Aleida or Celia, although Ernesto continued being one of my best friends. We saw each other less since he had returned from the USSR where he had spent five years studying law. He and I have always treated one another like brothers.

Later I thought that perhaps I should have crashed Aleida's wedding and before the toast to the bride I should have stood up and asked her if she had fought against any injustice that week, and when she answered that she hadn't had an opportunity to see any injustice except for an undeserved failing grade on one of her friend's exams in medical school, say to her:

"Don't you think that the people in prison for disagreeing with the government present a sufficient injustice to compel you to banish this monster from your wedding—this bearded man you call your Uncle Fidel, and if he refuses to leave, to do so yourself?"

And after that I would have calmly gone to my apartment packed my bags and resigned myself to the fate of leaving on a direct flight for Siberia in Russia, where so many Cubans who behaved erratically were sent to spend a season during the time of Brezhnev's rule. But I didn't crash her wedding.

It was not my intention to hurt Jenny, but I would have liked to tell her that perhaps her grandfather the president committed suicide because of the constant disdain he was subjected to by the men who had fought in the Sierra Maestra, the men who, influenced by Fidel's point of view that men who had not been a part of the fight were less than imitations of frogs or mice, treated Dorticós as inferior to themselves. I would have liked to express my doubts about whether Dorticós committed suicide only because his wife had died and he didn't want to live without her in his utter loneliness without the only witness of all that had occurred, but prior to her death something must have emptied his life of purpose in such a way that with her gone, life made no sense to him.

I would have told her that, as I saw it, both her grandfather and my uncle had been used by Fidel in whatever way had suited him, and then he had cast them away, first by taking away their positions in government, turning them into occupants of an empty space that impeded their breathing—a space belonging to no one, or better yet, to a dead man. To a dead hero, in the case of my uncle, and to a dead failure because he chose suicide and because he had never fired a shot in the Sierra, in the case of her grandfather.

I never said anything to Jenny because I didn't want to have all my friends worried about what the next words to come out of my mouth would be, words devoid of tenderness, and also because at that time I had not formed my thoughts well enough to express them. In addition, the time had not yet come when I would find out about the myriad atrocities that the Revolutionary government had committed in the name of the good of humanity.

Chapter Twenty-Five

I believe that the dilemma of fight or flight in Fidel's Cuba was resolved most of the time by flight. Not so much out of cowardice or fear to fight against injustice, but because of the belief that flight was a way of betraying Fidel without confronting the man that they believed had provided them with an education and free health care, and given them freedom and dignity in the face of North America, and they could not pay him back fighting against him or against all those who had screamed "*¡Patria o Muerte!*" ("Country or Death!") in the Plaza of the Revolution, much in the same way than when a Christian feels that the Church has betrayed him, that there is no God waiting to listen to the prayers of the faithful, and that Christ is no longer on the cross but on a yacht, and alienates himself from his beliefs and the liturgy that meant so much to him, he will not blaspheme or take God by the neck and drown him in a toilet. It is something stronger than anger, than certainty, than conviction. It is the fear of offending the Father forever, with no hope for turning back.

I have seen many men, hostages of the Revolution, exhibit an alliance to their captors. Some, after serving years in prison expressing that they had been wrong and that they should be more like revolutionaries, that their punishment had been just. The people in their great majority even knowing all had gone wrong and that the path had been corrupted, knowing they were heading toward the abyss, continued to march, slowly but without pause towards their final destiny consuming more quantities of rum of lesser quality.

Here was the Stockholm Syndrome under the Caribbean sun, an encompassing and collective disease that perhaps infected me a little differently than others.

We hailed a cab, I offered the driver ten pesos above his fare and he agreed to drive us home. On the way home, Mariana fell asleep with her head on my shoulder. I thought about the exhausting day I'd had. Some of my friends who would go to work each day to spend eight hours doing nothing except talking to their friends about baseball or talking to their family on the telephone would ask if I had a job yet. When they saw me on the street they would say: "Hey, Martín, how are you? Always the good life, eh? When are you going to get a job?" I thought I worked harder without a job than they did with a job.

We arrived at The Siberia, our neighborhood in Alamar, and the cab dropped us off before reaching the apartment. Cabs didn't want to risk getting their wheels stuck in the holes in the pavement or in the mud, and always dropped us off about a hundred meters from our building. Mariana had no choice but to wake up.

The next morning we got up late. It was Saturday and my brother and sister didn't have to go school. I went to the pizzeria to buy a few pizzas, soft drinks, and beer. It was a beautiful day and water was even flowing from the faucets.

My sister Ana went to pre-university classes at Antonio Guiteras School in El Vedado. She had to catch a bus every morning, and most days she just managed to find a spot precariously hanging on to the side of it. She was frequently late. My brother had the same problem when he rode to the Instituto Superior de Arte, somewhat further away.

Their lives were orderly and they behaved well. They studied, and they didn't share my ideas about the society in which we lived. Lucky for them they didn't share my attitude! They had and have a life much different than mine. They are really good people and I don't want to mention them more than I already have. I will only say that the Council of State through the office of Fidel's secretary cared for all three of us. They each received a stipend of seventy pesos every month that I was denied. Every month they had to go and pick up their money. Sometimes Sonia, Chomi's secretary, would ask them to encourage me to go to Chomi's office as soon as possible. When they told me I would think to myself: "Why, after all these years when you have been denied a stipend and an education, why does it make you feel good when you receive these invitations?"

My son Alejandro had been born a few months back and every time I could I would make time to go see him. He had come into the world under not very favorable circumstances. This child that in his baby universe must have wanted a father and a mother that loved him and were by his side, had the love of his parents but only the daily care of his mother. I could see no way to change that no matter how much the thought hurt me or how much I wished it did.

He was not Mariana's son. He was conceived during a three-month time in which Mariana and I had broken up after which we came together with a stronger commitment but with this small problem. During the three months of our breakup I had started seeing an old girlfriend from my pre-university days in Miramar with whom I had maintained a good relationship. We spent a few days together and during that time she became pregnant. I knew it was only a matter of time before I went back to the arms of my real love Mariana whom I missed terribly, so I saw several girls during that time, knowing my freedom to do so wouldn't last. I had a good time, but once I went back to Mariana, besides fearing a knock at the door from the Council of State I had dreams of several women in various stages of pregnancy coming through my door and saying loudly: "Yes, you are the father, you are, but don't worry, your duty as a good father is to flee."

Mariana had a very hard time with Alejandrito's birth. I felt guilty for having caused a wound in her that would be hard if not impossible to heal. For that reason, every time I went to see my son I told her I was going but I tried to go alone. She would say no, that she wanted to see him too, that if she loved me she should be able to bear seeing that child. The first time she saw him was on Fifth Avenue in Miramar. I picked him up at his mother's house and when I brought him close to her she leaned in. My son was asleep, his rosy cheeks on my shoulder. Mariana said:

"He looks like a little version of you, Martín."

She looked me in the eyes then her pupils dilating, and I could see the depth of the woman who I almost possessed, who had allowed me to be a part of her, but a woman whom I had refused to fully take into my heart, into myself. I had preferred to decline the privilege. I wasn't sure at that moment whether I was more touched by the sight of my son in my arms or by the generosity of Mariana's spirit.

Every day of our lives Mariana proved she was capable of more love than I. But that day she had shown me she was in a totally separate league. But it was not because of Alejandro that our love began to wane since that day, although we stayed together for some time, but because of a sensation that I was invading and corrupting her, this woman who far from me had the possibility of a better life, of being more loved and doubtlessly of being treated with more respect. Perhaps it was the noblest thing I did for her, to begin to flood my eyes with a dark inscrutable ocean that she could not penetrate, an ocean that anyone who dared enter would drown. I watched her distance herself from me with an acute ache in my heart.

Chapter Twenty-Six

The regime had done all they could to squash artistic creativity that did not pay homage to the church of Marxist-Leninist thought. Despite their efforts, young people were beginning to join the ranks of the rebel artists of Cuba, a more important development than the existence of a few of the old ones.

I sat at a bar in the UNEAC called El Hurón Azúl (The Blue Heron) located on the side of the building. It was bordered by framboyán trees and adorned with tables and chairs made of rod iron and painted in white. Someone started to play the piano and my friend Blanca joined me. At times Blanca offered me more than her friendship, and we had a very comfortable relationship as friends with benefits. We passed the time drinking and reminiscing, and soon Leonardo Acosta, a well-known musician who was the author of several books and a good source of knowledge about music, joined us.

We launched into a conversation about North American Jazz and how Cuban percussion had enriched it, when Chano

Pozo played with Dizzy Gillespie and after Mongo Santamaría had sought refuge in the United States. Leonardo was very knowledgeable in reference to the history of jazz. I asked him if Rock and Roll was the most developed form of rhythmic expression. He smiled and said, "Rock can be a lot of fun, Martín, but it's in a league of its own." He recommended I listen to Keith Jarret. I wrote the name on a piece of paper, paid our bill, and went to buy a pizza at La Piragua, next to the Hotel Nacional, where I found a table outside to sit and eat while enjoying the fresh air across from the Malecón.

I asked for a pizza to go and walked to the Hotel Nacional to drink rum in the lower-level bar while listening to some good music. Tonight, a pianist was playing and I relaxed until I almost fell asleep.

The sight of an attractive woman with large breasts who had seated herself near me brought me fully awake. I flirted with her and went to sit at her table. I bought her a drink but was unsuccessful in my mission to get her to have sex with me. She was staying at the hotel and had come from the province of Matanzas to Havana for the Camilo-Che celebrations. I told her I was Che's nephew but I didn't want to talk about the festivities. That brought her closer to me physically and her flirty behavior increased, but in the end she told me that although she found me attractive, she was part of a large delegation at the hotel. She was married and afraid someone would see us together and tell her husband about us when she went home. I thanked her, kissed her hand, got up, and left.

I was absolutely monogamous. I never had a serious relationship with two women at the same time. That would have seemed like a betrayal. But I wasn't faithful. I only loved Mariana, and loved her with all my heart. There was no room in my heart for anyone else. But I was more generous with parts of my body other than my heart, and open to any possibility.

Once I left the hotel I felt lightheaded and somewhat guilty knowing my behavior would have hurt Mariana. I walked to the Hotel Capri and there I continued to drink enough rum to ensure I would get drunk, straight rum, no ice.

When I left the Hotel Capri I could feel myself weaving as I walked and the setting sun on my face intensified my feeling of drunkenness. It wasn't unusual to see a drunk weaving through the streets of Cuba or holding on to a telephone pole in any corner. I arrived at Twenty Third and L and headed to the Habana Libre Hotel to drink some more. I couldn't drink much more because everything around me felt like it was going in circles, but I wanted a couple of more drinks before going to sleep at home in Mariana's arms. When I arrived at the door of the hotel that had been my home for so many years, everything around me faded and I fell unconscious to the floor. I came to in an ambulance near the hotel. There was a very thin man seated by me. He was of medium height and had the look of an intellectual. He told me he knew who I was. I wondered how he could know something that was so complicated that I myself did not know, but he was referring to something much more trivial, my being a Guevara, one of the tribe of Unga Dunga chiefs, a blue-blood with red stripes because of communism. He only knew that I was Che's nephew, yet he said he knew "who" I was, and every time he looked at me I could see him comparing me with his preconceived ideas of how a relative of my uncle's should act. But this man was different. His voice carried no trace of reproach. He appeared willing to listen and understand. He asked me if I felt well yet and I told him that I was feeling many things, some hard to explain, but well wasn't one of them.

The man told me that I had passed out at the entrance to the hotel and the guards standing near the door had tried to help me. He had identified himself as a doctor, went to get some water, and asked the guards to call an ambulance thinking that I might have had a heart attack or a stroke.

It hadn't been necessary to check my pocket for identification because two men who worked at the hotel recognized me. They didn't remember my name, but they remembered my pedigree. The man introduced himself. He was Doctor Pujol, the director of a mental health clinic, the CENSAM, located in Jaimanitas. He explained that most people who were staying at the CENSAM were alcoholics. He told me that the doors of his clinic were open to me and that if I decided to go, even for a visit, I would be welcome. He said it would be his honor and his pleasure to help me.

I couldn't remember the last time anyone had been so nice to me outside of my close circle of friends, and I was puzzled, almost annoyed that anyone would be that interested in me, in my recovery, in my mental health. It was the first time anyone had spoken to me that way, and he was a complete stranger.

In that moment I was overcome by religious sentiment. I thought Babalú Ayé, the Yoruba deity that according to that religion cures the sick, was sending him to me. Almost every time I got drunk, I sang the song of praise and respect to that saint whom I had been introduced to in the neighborhood of Regla, in what was known as a *"plante."* It was only in Regla that white men were allowed to witness the Yoruba ceremonies. E-cua, e-cua; Babalú Ayé, ecua.

Like Jorge Luis Borges, I didn't believe in coincidences. I thought that all things happened by design although we may not recognize where they come from or their purpose. One way or another, the fact that there was a man sitting across from me who appeared to be knowledgeable, self-assured and compassionate and was the head of an excellent clinic, and that he was inviting me to be his patient, was exactly what I needed at that moment in time.

When he made a comment that he suspected that I had passed out due to the immense burden of symbolism I carried on that eighth of October, I laughed inside my head because it was so obvious. It would have been better for me if I had not taken him lightly. I thanked him for his help trying to speak coherently enough for him to understand me. The world was still reeling around me and I wished that this man would never leave my side, and that the ambulance would stay in front of the door of the Habana Libre with me inside it forever.

Before leaving he told me one more thing: that the clinic he was in charge of was a beautiful place, with pools and squash courts. He gave me a card with his name, his phone number, and the address of his clinic.

When I felt better the next day, I told Mariana what had happened. It was obvious I needed treatment, but I didn't want to admit how much. I searched my mind to find excuses that would make it okay for me to spend some time in a madhouse. I found two.

My mother and grandmother had decided to return to Cuba after my mother lost her job in Buenos Aires, where she had been the director of publicity for a magazine called *Video News*. She received a great severance package and was afraid she would go through her money before she could find another job she liked. She thought about that and about the widow's pension my grandmother received, and came to the conclusion that with the help of the Council of State she could live very well in the island of infinite queues ruled by Fidel's whims. Going to the clinic could facilitate a transition for me. By the time I was released, my mother would have requested housing from the Council of State and she would have been given a large-enough place for her and for my grandmother to live in.

The second reason was that my going to the clinic might placate Chomi, who would now see that I was not a perennial partygoer or a lazy citizen, but someone who was a little touched in the head.

I went to see Doctor Pujol that day. I took a cab. When the driver asked my destination and I said I was going to the CENSAM he asked who I was going to see. I told him I was going to see the director and asked him why he wanted to know. He said the only people interned there were generals, officials of the NININT, Ministers of State, or their immediate families. I thought that if that was the case it might be a nice place.

The cab left me at the entrance. I was in Jaimanitas, near the house of Fidel and his body-guards, near ground zero. The clinic was a complex of new buildings, chalets, and cabins, adorned by gardens and traversed by the Jaimanitas River that flowed into the ocean.

I arrived at Doctor Pujol's office. He greeted me with a warm handshake and some hot coffee. He explained that my treatment would consist of rest and medication with time in individual and group therapy. There would be scheduled exercise, the opportunity to watch movies, as well as a lot of free time. He said the majority of the patients had come from jobs that had intensive schedules, and I thought that many were probably deeply affected because the injustices they had been forced to witness and the things they had been asked to do.

We went for a long walk and Doctor Pujol explained the layout and the purpose of each building. We passed men and women in pajamas that who walked with arms akimbo like zombies, apparently overmedicated. They lived in a section reserved for those who were coming back from armed conflicts in which Cuba was involved, the so-called International Missions that differed from Imperialist missions only in the prefix of the words

Imperialist and International. He explained to me that one of the men there had lost his hands and his eyes in a grenade explosion in Africa and that the woman who leading him by his arm was his mother. His wife had left him shortly after he returned because she could not deal with his injuries. He asked me not to worry, that I would not be living in this section.

I would be in a cabin next to the river, in close proximity to the swimming pool, the billiard table, and the birdcages, where I would have a large room with air conditioning all to myself. When I saw where I would be staying, I waited a moment to tell him, "Yes, doctor, I'll stay." But I had paused only because I didn't want to seem too eager. I had taken in the beauty of a place where I could breathe in an incredible sense of peace. In the few moments I had spent there, I had already started to feel better.

He led me to the main house, a white house with a marble swimming pool flanked by two statues of lions that stood at alert, ready to attack. It was obvious that the house had been constructed before the Revolution, because its quality was superior to the structures that had been constructed after the Revolution. Doctor Pujol said, "Martín, this main house was the original structure here. At one time before it was a clinic, it was the property of Al Capone, the famous Mafioso."

I was already sure I wanted to stay, but that detail convinced me to do so. I agreed to stay there for the next few months. We went to the dining room that smelled like a five-star restaurant and he asked me to join him for lunch. I agreed to do so. We shook hands in agreement and I ate my lunch. The next day I returned to the clinic taking with me my suitcase and some personal effects. Mariana was not totally happy, but the possibility that I might stop drinking and settle into a more peaceful life gave her a reason to support my decision with some modicum of enthusiasm. After a time I would be allowed to spend weekends at home.

I didn't for one moment think I would stop drinking, but I was looking forward to a good rest and to some self-examination that might help me discover why I always managed to fail in all my attempts to incorporate myself into society. I hadn't found the answer before, so I had nothing to lose by trying Al Capone. After all, he was another public enemy of the United States. Perhaps seeing him in that light, might Fidel have considered him, had he lived, a friend of the Revolution? Al Capone, the Capo of the Mafia, worthy therapist for the madness of real socialism and scientific communism.

Three months into my idyllic stay, I was expelled from the clinic after being discovered drinking the night away with some of the nurses.

Chapter Twenty-Seven

I spent the night in a jail cell with little notion of where I was. When a police car took me home my mother said:

"Martín, you are going to destroy us all!"

And so it was that she spoke with the Council of State and my father, so they would invite me to abandon the island. In a week I was returning to Argentina along with my cousin Camilo, Che's son, who was headed to Buenos Aires to participate in various functions related to the anniversary of his father's death. We were going back for different reasons, chatting amicably in a Boeing of Cubana de Aviacion headed for the country that Che had run away from.

My girlfriend Mariana had left me at the clinic and gone back to Chile, her native country. My cousins hardly acknowledged me when they saw me on the street. My mother, my siblings, even my grandmother wanted me to go far away, somewhere where I could continue my self-destruction so they didn't have to reinvent the black sheep or be bothered by my proximity to them. I wondered why I would ever miss Cuba.

I had left a land where people who believed in Fidel when he said he wanted a better world, offered to him their youth, the best years of their life. People traveled to other countries to give of themselves without pay inspired by an idea; I left a country where the most hopeful intentions were sown in a unique beginning for a Latin American country. Those intentions were truncated almost immediately with the total repression against any difference with its content and form.

Here there was repression through imprisonment, death, and exile, but the most brutal of all to the people who gave the revolution wings, who responded with their work but were ostracized, was the destiny of alcoholism, madness or dissentsion on the one hand, or total servitude on the other.

The Revolution does not allow partial slavery. It squeezes the human being so hard that it leaves no room even for self-esteem.

I had a Cuban son, Cuban cousins, Cuban friends, but I had something else that was Cuban: the capacity to survive everything—perhaps not with the grace of the native Cubans, but with the purpose of enjoying every moment.

A popular Cuban joke says that if there is a nuclear catastrophe, the only species that will survive will be the cockroach and the Cuban, not necessarily in that order.

To survive whatever might come with good taste and total skepticism after so many years of lies: I can't imagine a greater legacy for today's world.

The socialist messianic message, the damage caused by the incursion into arrogance and extremism in leftist politics destroyed the possibility of a free world, a society without imposition, where liberty of intellect, artistic liberty, and, above all, personal freedom, could exist.

The consciousness of violence, the idea that crime in any of its manifestations will help us attain our goals, will only take us back to the place we wanted to escape from in the first place. I rested my head feeling myself being lulled into sleep by the drone of the engine that was carrying me to Argentina. Suddenly my mind wandered back to the night when I met Fidel at the fair. That night I said to him:

"Fidel, I am Juan Martín Guevara's son. He has been taken prisoner in Argentina. I know you and my uncle were best friends. Will you help to free my father?"

Fidel met my eyes and said: "I will see to it that he comes home very soon. I give you my promise as a Revolutionary."

Chapter Twenty-Eight

One day like any other in October, my uncle Che fell on the ground of a small rural school in Yuro, Bolivia, his body riddled with bullets, his ribs visible through his skin, blood covering his chest now ravaged by starvation and asthma. He had become a much smaller man with so little sustenance, but he was still feared. He fell with his eyes open, alert to his last breath, to the images that formed his last thoughts and remained suspended in the ether until he began his journey towards the people that mattered to him who had taken this journey before him. His last day coincided with the last days of his guerrilla movement. He was practically alone. It was a brutal loneliness that contrasted sharply with the objective he desired: to create various hot-spots of guerrilla warfare in all of Latin America, or, at a minimum, to start a Revolution in Bolivia. But he was alone, as he had sometimes longed to be. Man yearns to confront that which he most fears. The abyss calls the man who suffers vertigo and whom his drugs seduce, the addict. Che had gone far in his game. He had been able to experience his mother's death before his own and

Shadow of a Myth

now knew he could die far away from his own without caring about the Cuban Revolution or even the current one he was involved in since he recognized that the adventure's end approached. At that point revolutions were only as important as Pepto Bismol was to the stomach after eating buttered sausage or greasy fish-and-chips. After my uncle said goodbye to Fidel and to his own children in Havana, he went to Africa where he was not very successful as the leader of a new revolutionary movement, although he did manage to recruit Laurent Kabila, the guerrilla leader of the Belgian Congo, in his fight against Mobutu, who had recently taken power after a coup d'état. Uncle Che had to end his association with Kabila because he had no discipline or ethics. He said "nothing allows me to think that Kabila is the right man for this moment." Thirty years later, Kabila would defeat Mobutu, having allied himself with other guerrilla leaders and assume the mantel of power like a new little king prohibiting political parties, getting rid of most all newspapers that were not aligned with his philosophy, and relentlessly pursuing all who opposed his new regime. A few days after Che left for Africa, Fidel gathered thousands in the Plaza of the Revolution and in front of a multitude of citizens proceeded to read a letter written that was to be read in the event of his death. I believe that Fidel, adroit as he was in the art of intrigue, read that letter in public, published it in the two national newspapers, and had it read through intercoms in every workplace, to guarantee that whether Che triumphed or failed, he would never return to be an influence on the government of Cuba. When Che learned that the letter had been read prior to his death, he felt a wave of disillusionment.

In 1966, my grandmother Celia died asking herself why her beloved son didn't answer her last letters or come to say goodbye to her before she passed, holding her as she had done him during those first fifteen days of his life when he almost died from asthma. When Che found out his mother died without learning he had left Cuba, he was filled with angst and anger and wrote a beautiful poem titled "The Stone."

Uncle Che wrote some beautiful poems, some were truly exceptional. He spent a few months in a town called Ladvi, forty miles south of Prague, recovering from severe asthma. There he also wrote about the subject of economics and politics. He was disappointed in the direction the USSR was taking, for the way of the life of the poor there.

Another reason he stayed in Ladvi for so long was that it afforded him an opportunity to spend more time with Tamara Bunker, with whom he was planning his next guerrilla activities in Bolivia. Some think that in addition to the adventure in Bolivia they also actively participated in their own. The place was conducive to comfort, to the marriage of work and pleasure. The truth of that liaison is not known.

What is known is that the maternal love that had infused him with so much energy through the distance of miles and years, had come to an end. The Bolivian project started out flawed from the beginning. I see that now looking at it in retrospect. The general secretary of the Bolivian Communist Party and my uncle could not come to an agreement about who would be in charge of the guerrilla movement. Neither wanted to abdicate their respective power and obviously Uncle Che had little ability in matters of persuasion. He ended up alone with his men in the jungles of Bolivia. He had the love and affection of many, but that was not enough to reach the objectives of a revolutionary war. About a year and some months after he and his men had arrived in Bolivia, little had changed. The authorities had been intensively searching for him for weeks. Little by little his men were killed and no new recruits joined the guerrilla movement in the Bolivian jungle. Fidel wasn't there, the great orator that persuaded men that an oak was a spruce, through his power of prestidigitation. Uncle Che told the people the truth about what to expect in a guerrilla war and what to expect of him as their very demanding leader. He also told them he had little tolerance for laziness and gluttony. That, along with his inability to negotiate strategic alliances, put him in a situation that I suspected was the one he wanted to be in, given that he described himself with warm affection and self-appreciation as a solitary man. A few weeks before being taken into custody, Che's men had dwindled down to just a few bearded, rifle-carrying, starving men. Men who would never speak out loud about their hunger, and who would not accept even in the innermost recesses of their being, the image of a banquet as their only object of desire. But now as death grew closer, they could think of no victory except that of filling their stomachs in the face of hunger provoked by the nearness of death. But not my uncle.

It was as if his view of himself altered. As if he was becoming the image that he pursued and feared for so long, when he long ago had baptized his horse Rocinante and made friends with a pipe in the style of Jack London. This time, unlike in his time in the Sierra with Fidel when he smoked his Rothschild cigars, he appeared to have re-encountered in himself the man who loved book sales, the winner of rugby games despite his asthma; he seemed to have dismissed the days as an implacable minister, as an intolerant with no room in himself for the lyrical. In his last days, he thought more about relieving the toothache of a man than of executing one of his men over a disagreement. The hunger in his stomach began to liberate him of other burdens. It was the only way he could feel good atop Rocinante, right before colliding with the windmills. Hunger and the certainty that he would not leave that jungle alive allowed him to stop thinking of revolutions without feeling guilt, and to enjoy a few days of unencumbered and almost peaceful life before leaving the world of the asthmatics.

Epilogue

It was the eighth of October, the beginning of the celebration of Camilo-Che, that began on the anniversary of Che's death and lasted until the twenty-eighth of the month, the anniversary of the day in 1959 when Camilo Cienfuegos, a major hero of the Revolution beloved hero of the Cuban people, disappeared under very mysterious circumstances. The celebration of Camilo-Che was like a Revolutionary version of Lent, a time of Revolutionary reflection when feasts and concerts and memorials celebrated the life of my uncle Che and his friend and comrade in the Sierra Maestra, Camilo Cienfuegos.

Cuban Newspapers dedicated pages upon pages to exalting the super-human qualities of the dead heroes. Mornings in the schools grew interminable, filled with talks and activities centered around Che and Camilo. During those twenty days The Committees for the Defense of the Revolution organized meetings that people knew better than to miss, in order to read works that referenced the two commanders. These meetings were a great opportunity for a citizen who had a small infraction against the government in his history to earn some brownie points by praising the country's heroes in a louder voice than his neighbors.

On the last day of the celebration, in the morning, all the children of all the schools were taken to the Malecón, or to another beach, to make a floral offering to Camilo at the seaside. The seaside was chosen because the official and unbelievable story stated that his airplane had crashed into the ocean on a day totally devoid of clouds, after his meeting with Commander Huber Matos in which he relayed Fidel's order to the Commander to give himself up. Huber Matos immediately agreed and Camilo disappeared, leaving Fidel with single ownership of the Cuban people's heart. At the end of the day, Fidel ended the celebration with a typically long speech that was transmitted by both television channels and almost all radio stations, and re-transmitted the next day for those unable to go to the Plaza to listen to their leader, to wave a few flags, yell a few cheers, and spend a few hours in the waning October sun. Then, as was customary, a few epic poems of the Revolution were read. People left their seats politely, careful not to make much noise, and fled courteously from the boredom of the sonnets. I left with them, ready for a beer or rum on the rocks with lemon, and dreaming of the land the old Cubans spoke about where people didn't starve and ate all the ham and steak they wished.

www.ingramcontent.com/pod-product-compliance
Lightning Source LLC
Chambersburg PA
CBHW031953080426
42735CB00007B/371